Second Edition

Skillful 3

Reading & Writing Student's Book

Authors: Louis Rogers and Dorothy E. Zemach
Series Consultant: Dorothy E. Zemach

Grammar	Writing	Study skills	Unit outcomes
Use reflexive pronouns	Practice methods of brainstorming Plan, write, and edit an essay debating whether personality changes over time	Self-awareness and self-evaluation	Recognize and understand classification in texts Recognize substitution words to understand what they refer to Brainstorm and compose an essay
Use *can* for universal truths	Practice organizing ideas Write an essay discussing the advantages of handmade products over machine-made products	Writing a first draft	Recognize and understand the technique of internal paraphrasing in texts Understand exemplification to support an argument Compose and edit an essay using reasons and examples to support your argument
Use adverbs to hedge the strength of statements	Practice organizing a compare-and-contrast essay Write an essay comparing and contrasting the importance of emotional and intellectual intelligence	Improving memory through association and mnemonics	Recognize and understand the use of ellipsis in texts Understand the function of questions in texts Organize and compose a compare-and-contrast essay
Use gerunds and reduced clauses	Practice developing your arguments with supporting information Write a problem / solution essay on wildfires	Smart reading	Recognize and use word parts to understand meaning Recognize sentence modifiers to identify point of view Brainstorm and compose a problem / solution essay
Use the future passive	Practice describing plans and predictions in the future Write a comparison essay of two maps	Set your priorities	Practice using annotations to understand a text Recognize and understand text structure Brainstorm and compose a comparison of two maps

Grammar	Writing	Study skills	Unit outcomes
Use conditionals with *provided* and *unless*	Practice writing definitions for essays Write a cause-and-effect essay on research into disease	Use feedback from your tutors	Recognize and understand paragraph structure Practice identifying sentence functions Compose and edit a cause-and-effect essay
Use the present perfect progressive	Practice inferring reasons for change Write a description summarizing and comparing trends in animal populations shown on a graph and infer reasons for the changes	Avoiding self-sabotage	Practice identifying support for opinions Recognize and use research questions Brainstorm and compose a description of a graph
Use unreal conditionals in the past	Practice writing and supporting an essay thesis Write a for or against essay on speaking out about unethical colleagues	Argumentative writing	Practice activating prior knowledge Practice summarizing sections of a text Compose and edit a for or against essay
Use defining and non-defining relative clauses	Practice varying sentence length in explanations Write an essay on technology	Identifying what gets good marks	Understand and practice creating a text map Practice taking notes to understand key ideas Brainstorm and compose an essay
Use future perfect simple	Practice identifying and writing a stance for an opinion essay Write an opinion essay	Overcoming writer's block	Identify and understand conclusions Recognize and understand text predictions Compose and edit an opinion essay

To the student

Academic success requires so much more than memorizing facts. It takes skills. This means that a successful student can both learn and think critically.

Skillful gives you:

- Skills you need to succeed when reading and listening to academic texts
- Skills you need to succeed when writing for and speaking to different audiences
- Skills for critically examining the issues presented by a speaker or a writer
- Study skills for learning and remembering the English language and important information.

To successfully use this book, use these strategies:

Come to class prepared to learn. This means that you should show up well fed, well rested, and prepared with the proper materials. Watch the video online and look at the discussion point before starting each new unit.

Ask questions and interact. Learning a language is not passive. You need to actively participate. Help your classmates, and let them help you. It is easier to learn a language with other people.

Practice! Memorize and use new language. Use the *Skillful* online practice to develop the skills presented in the Student's Book. Revise vocabulary on the review page.

Review your work. Look over the skills, grammar, and vocabulary from previous units. Study a little bit each day, not just before tests.

Be an independent learner, too. Look for opportunities to study and practice English outside of class, such as reading for pleasure and using the Internet in English. Remember that learning skills, like learning a language, takes time and practice. Be patient with yourself, but do not forget to set goals. Check your progress and be proud of your success! I hope you enjoy using *Skillful*!

Dorothy E. Zemach – Series Consultant

Opening page

Each unit starts with two opening pages. These pages get you ready to study the topic of the unit. There is a video to watch and activities to do before you start your class.

Reading lessons

In every unit, there are two reading lessons and they present two different aspects of the unit topic and help you with ideas and language for your writing task.

Vocabulary to prepare you for the reading activities.

Develop your reading skills in each part of the reading lesson.

Glossaries help you understand higher level words from the reading text.

Every reading section helps you use a new reading skill.

Writing lessons

After your reading lessons, there is a page for you to analyze a model answer to a writing task. This will help you organize your ideas and language and prepare for your final task at the end of the unit.

First, analyze the model answer.

Brainstorm and plan your final writing task.

Finally, write your paragraph or essay.

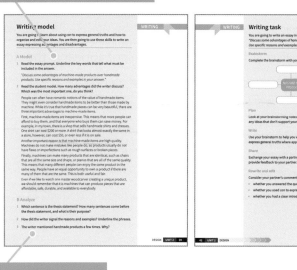

Next, discuss your ideas.

Discussion point

Discuss with a partner.

1 How do you display your identity in person?

   My clothes say a lot about me. I'm an athlete, so I wear …

2 How do you display your identity online?

   My screen name is pony98 because I love horses, and I was born in 1998. So, that shows …

3 Do you think your online identity is communicated accurately?

   I'm not sure. I post a lot of happy photos and good news. So, …

How I display my identity in person

How I display my identity online

clothes · tone of voice · what I say · gestures and body language

screen name · avatar · colors and fonts · photos · what I write

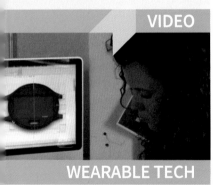

VIDEO

WEARABLE TECH

Before you watch

Work with a partner. Discuss how these words might appear in the video.

a gadget attached to your wrist   to feel alert

a fitness tracker   bio-data

rhythms and pulses   'wearable' technology

upbeat music   to be unique

UNIT AIMS

READING 1 Recognizing and understanding classification texts
READING 2 Recognizing substitution words
STUDY SKILL Self-awareness and self-evaluation

VOCABULARY Vocabulary to describe identity types
GRAMMAR Reflexive pronouns
WRITING Techniques for brainstorming

Standing out from the crowd.

While you watch

Read the questions. Watch the video and choose *T* (True) or *F* (False).

1 The gadget in the video is a watch.   T / F
2 It keeps you fit.   T / F
3 You wear it next to your pulse to link to
   your body's rhythms.   T / F
4 It works the same way musical rhythms
   affect your moods.   T / F
5 The gadget has to collect lots of bio-data
   via your phone.   T / F

After you watch

Discuss the questions with a partner.

1 Do you like the idea of a gadget that can change
   your moods?

   Yes, I do / No, I don't because …

2 Do you agree with the inventor that the gadget is
   unique?

   I agree. I think …

   No, I'm afraid I disagree because …

3 What gadget would you like to invent to improve
   your health?

   I'd like …

   I think … would be very …

Social identity

A Vocabulary preview

Complete the sentences with the words in the box.

categorize   confirmed   consequences
debate   define   desirable   mature   tensions

1   It is generally said that girls _Mature_ quicker than boys.
2   I think patience and loyalty are _desirable_ qualities in a friend.
3   Measures are needed to reduce _debate_ _tensious_ between fans at the next game.
4   She said exactly what she thought, without thinking about the _cousequeuces_
5   Happiness is a very difficult feeling to _define_.
6   The two psychologists had a _debate_ over the cause of the problem.
7   I _categorize_ my social media contacts into family, close friends, and work colleagues.
8   When I received an award for writing, that just _confirmed_ my desire to be a journalist.

B Before you read

Preparing to read

The reading discusses different types of groups that people belong to that form part of their identity and some of the traits, or characteristics, that they share. What kinds of examples do you think the reading mentions?

C Global reading

Recognizing classification

Classification is used in texts to talk about different types of something—for example, different breeds of horses or different stages of a child's development. Some texts will directly state the number of categories: *There are six major biomes in the North American landscape*. Other texts will give signals such as *First*, *In addition*, and *Finally* in the first or second sentence of the body paragraphs. Some texts will list the categories in the first or second paragraph: *The three main types of rock are known as sedimentary, metamorphic, and igneous*. Then you can expect one supporting paragraph to explain each category.

Write the headings in the box into the text. Remember to skim for topic sentences to help you.

Dangers of social identity   Implications
The importance of identity   Types of identity traits

Social identity

It's hard to imagine meeting someone for the first time and not exchanging any personal information. At the very least, you offer your name and a few important facts—perhaps age, occupation, reason for joining a certain organization, or reason for attending a certain class. As friendships develop, however, the answer to the question "Who are you?" becomes more complex.

Our identities start to form when we are children and continue to grow, solidify, and even change as we mature. A person's identity is actually made up of many different aspects, some broad and some narrow. For instance, you might identify with the broad categories of *German, male*, and *student* as well as the narrower ones of *violinist*, *left-handed person*, and *brother of Anna*.

1 _____

Identity traits can be ascribed, achieved, or chosen. An ascribed trait is one that you are born with; examples include your ethnicity, your birthplace, and being the child and possibly the sibling of certain people. An achieved trait is one you work for, such as being a university graduate or the employee of a certain company. An identity such as a club membership or affiliation with a political party is chosen.

However, traits are not always so easy to categorize. Is speaking your native language, for example, ascribed (because you were born into the family and country where that language was spoken), achieved (because you studied the language and became more proficient), or even chosen (if you grew up in a multilingual country, but preferred one language over another)?

2 _____

Our identities are important not only because they shape our belief in who we are, but also because they impact how others treat us.

Although traits can be positive (*intelligent*; *loyal*) or negative (*stubborn*; *criminal*), people are more affected by how similar or different their traits are compared to those of other people. For example, if you are a fan of the Falcons sports team, you have something in common with other Falcons fans.

The next time you go to an event or social gathering, watch how people who are strangers at first try to find something in common with the people they meet—perhaps a shared hometown, a similar occupation or hobby, or even the same opinion about the weather that day or a current event. Finding a shared identity helps people feel comfortable and accepted. If other people share a belief or characteristic, it's easier to believe that your feelings are correct or that your characteristics are desirable. That's a major reason why people form groups such as *citizens of Ankara* or *fans of Yao Ming* or *graduates of Springfield High School*.

3 _____

People don't just define themselves as who they are, however; they also define themselves as who they are not. That is to say, they aren't just *fans of the Springfield High School basketball team*; they are also **not** *fans of the Pleasant Valley High School basketball team*. A friendly rivalry between two sports teams isn't necessarily a bad thing, but when rivalries are taken too far or tensions arise over differences about larger social issues, the consequences can be more serious.

Interestingly, groups that have a lot in common sometimes form the most intense separate identities. To someone who doesn't use a computer at all, they might all seem very similar. However, debates over the best brands of laptop can become quite heated. People form different groups over whether they preferred a book or movie adaptation; which brand of cell phone they prefer; which leader in the same political party they support. States or cities that are near each other can be stronger rivals than those separated by greater distances. Rather than confirming the positive effects of social identity, these rivalries can make people feel insecure, threatened, angry, or even fearful.

4 _____

The challenge, then, for both leaders and all of us in society is to foster the positive effects of group membership while avoiding the negative ones.

GLOSSARY

affiliation (n) a connection with an organization

foster (v) to encourage or help something to develop

rivalry (n) a situation of intense competition between individuals or groups

sibling (n) a brother or sister

D Close reading

1 Find the definitions for the terms in *Social identity* and copy them, or express them in your own words.

1 ascribed trait: _____

2 achieved trait: _____

3 chosen trait: _____

2 Match the examples from the reading (1–9) with the concept they explain (a–i).

1	being the employee of a certain company	a	achieved trait
2	belonging to a political party	b	ascribed trait
3	stubborn; criminal	c	broad categories
4	fans of the Pleasant Valley High School team	d	chosen trait
5	intelligent; loyal	e	definition of something people are not
6	left-handed person	f	narrow categories
7	two different brands of laptops	g	negative traits
8	male; student	h	positive traits
9	brother of Anna	i	rivalries between different groups

E Critical thinking

Work with a partner. Discuss the questions.

1 What are some benefits of rivalries? What are some problems? Give specific examples.

2 When people meet for the first time, do you think they focus on similarities, or differences? Why, do you think?

3 Which of your identity traits do you think are the strongest: ascribed, achieved, or chosen? Do you think this is typical?

Study skills Self-awareness and self-evaluation

To develop a skill, you first need to know where you are starting from. What are your current strengths and weaknesses? What do you want to achieve? Where do you need to improve? What are your resources? What could obstruct your goals?

Ways of developing such awareness include:

- using self-evaluation questionnaires
- monitoring your progress
- maintaining a reflective journal or blog
- a group discussion or chat
- feedback from other students
- feedback and comments from teachers

© Stella Cottrell (2013)

1 Complete the chart with your own information about your study of English. Then share your responses with another student or a group.

My study of English

Goals	I want to be able to …
Strengths	I'm good at …
Weaknesses	I need to improve …
Aids (People and tools that can help me)	One thing that can help me is …
Challenges and obstacles	One thing that makes it difficult is …

2 Read the suggestions in the *Self-awareness and self-evaluation* box. Choose one or two methods that you would use to evaluate yourself in the following areas. Discuss your choices with a partner.

1 An artistic skill, such as singing, playing a musical instrument, or painting
2 An athletic skill, such as playing soccer, skiing, or dancing
3 Your performance at work / a job
4 Whether you should apply to a high-level university or graduate school

How permanent is your personality?

A Vocabulary preview

1 Match the words in bold with the correct definitions.

1	**correlation** (n)	a	happening now; at the present time
2	**current** (adj)	b	a person who takes part in a study or research
3	**frustrated** (adj)	c	to say that something is possible or likely; to imply
4	**modest** (adj)	d	not arrogant or vain; being quiet about one's abilities or achievements
5	**participant** (n)	e	a relationship or connection between two things
6	**rate** (v)	f	to be likely to happen; to be likely to do something
7	**suggest** (v)	g	to judge something or someone according to a scale; to grade
8	**tend to** (v)	h	upset, distressed, annoyed at a person or situation

2 Complete the sentences with words from Exercise 1. Change the form if necessary.

1 Is there any _____ between gender and personality traits?

2 I _____ be very careful about personal information I post online.

3 This study is really old. Do you know of a more _____ one?

4 When I don't understand something, even after the teacher has explained it twice, I feel _____.

5 The results of my research _____ that identity is important in all cultures in the world.

6 The survey was sent to over 1,000 people, but unfortunately, only about half of the _____ completed it correctly.

7 The applicant was _____ very high in technical skills, but rather low in social skills.

8 Although she won the competition, Sara didn't brag about it to her friends because she was a very _____ person.

Preparing to read

B Before you read

The title of this article asks a question: "How permanent is your personality?" What do you think is the answer to this question? Why?

Understanding main ideas

C Global reading

Skim *How permanent is your personality?* Is the tone formal or informal? How do you know? Who do you think is the intended audience?

How permanent is your personality?

1 You know the old saying: *You can't teach an old dog new tricks.* It's no surprise that we tend to believe that a person's personality is stable. People might disagree about whether someone is born with a certain personality or develops a personality while growing up, but it's commonly accepted that someone's personality will be much the same at age 50 as it was at age 20. Both in our personal lives and our work lives, we're told that we need to accept people the way they are and to learn to get along with other people even when they're difficult. After all, they're never going to change.

2 New evidence, however, suggests that this isn't true. Published in the journal *Psychology and Aging*, a comprehensive study by four psychologists examined a group of Scottish volunteers over a period of 63 years, making it the longest study of its type ever done. And what they found was unexpected: namely, no correlation at all between the participants' scores on personality tests when they were 14 years old and the same tests when they were 77 years old.

3 The test examined six areas: self-confidence, perseverance, stability of moods, conscientiousness, originality, and desire to learn. The original study involved 1,208 children, and 174 of them were available for the follow-up study six decades later. Because it's not reliable to have people rate themselves, the participants were evaluated in these categories by other people—by teachers when they were 14, and by friends or relatives when they were 77. They were also tested for intelligence and general well-being.

4 The researchers were surprised to find that none of the ratings matched up with each other over the years.

5 Earlier studies and tests produced somewhat different outcomes. Research suggested a few character traits had a low correlation over time and others had a modest correlation. The Scottish study, although smaller in scope because it involved fewer participants, measured them over a much longer period of time. This led the researchers to conclude that personality shifts are more likely to occur over long periods of time.

6 Now, it's not a perfect study, of course; such a thing is rare, if not impossible, with human beings and personality. For instance, the people who did the ratings in 1950 were not the same people who did the ratings in 2012, and this could have caused some difference. It's difficult for a study on something as broad as identity and personality to take all the variables into consideration. However, the results are still significant, and they have interesting implications.

7 Let's consider some of those implications for a moment. What does it all mean? And is it only of academic interest, or can you yourself apply this knowledge to your own life?

8   For one thing, it should give you a new way to think about other people. For example, say you're contacted on social media by someone you knew in school years ago. If you didn't like the person at that time, you might be tempted to refuse the connection. If you didn't like each other then, after all, why would you like each other now? But if it's true that personality can change, then there's a reason to give that person another chance. He or she might be very different now—and you might be too.

9   You might also have more reasonable expectations of old childhood friends who reconnect after many years. If you know their personalities (and yours) could have changed over the years, you'll be less disappointed if your friendship isn't as deep now as it was before. Rather than feel frustrated with yourselves, the two of you can accept that you have changed.

10   The study has implications for the workplace too. Personality forms a large part of a worker's suitability for a job, both in dealing with co-workers and in dealing with clients. If a person has a personality trait that interferes with work—say he argues with customers or she misses deadlines—it's important for managers to know that these traits can change. It's usually cheaper to train a current employee than to let that person go and hire a replacement. Even employees who aren't experiencing problems can be trained to be even better and more effective in terms of personality. This will help ensure that people continue to get along with one another.

11   Finally, there are personal implications. If you're the sort of person who says things like "I have a quick temper" or "My problem is I can't help procrastinating" or "I've always been too sensitive, and I blame myself whenever something goes wrong," it should be good news to know that these personality traits are not ones you have to keep. Although some therapists do good work helping patients accept themselves as they are, to build self-esteem, wouldn't it be more beneficial to eliminate negative personality traits than to learn to accept them? Knowing that you can change is the first stage in learning how to change. Then you can look forward to saying things like "I used to be too sensitive, but I'm not anymore"; to look forward to a time when, as we might start saying, you can learn some new tricks.

D Close reading

> *Other* can be an adjective or a noun. Only the noun can be plural:
>
> adjective   noun   plural noun
> *I prefer the **other** book. / I like this book better than **the other** / **the others**.*
>
> *Another* can be a determiner or a pronoun. Only the determiner is followed by a noun:
>
> determiner   pronoun
> *I'd like **another** book. / May I have **another**?*
>
> ***Each other*** and ***one another*** refer to two or more people at the same time. Use ***each other*** for two people, and ***one another*** for more than two:
> *The two students exchanged papers with **each other**.*
> *The children gave gifts to **one another**.* (We know there are three or more children).

Find examples of the substitution words from the box in *How permanent is your personality?* What are they referring to? Use the paragraph numbers to help you.

1 Paragraph 1: word or phrase: _____*other*_____
   refers to: *people to get along with* _____

2 Paragraph 4: word or phrase: _____
   refers to: _____

3 Paragraph 8: word or phrase: _____
   refers to: _____

4 Paragraph 8: word or phrase: _____
   refers to: _____

5 Paragraph 8: word or phrase: _____
   refers to: _____

6 Paragraph 10: word or phrase: _____
   refers to: _____

E Critical thinking

Work in a group. Discuss the questions.

1 Did the results of the study surprise you? Why / why not? Do you believe the results?

2 What are some factors that could cause someone to change his or her personality?

3 What do you think the results of this study imply for ascribed, achieved, and chosen identity traits? Can they all change, do you think? Why / why not?

Vocabulary development

Vocabulary for identity types

Both scientists and amateurs use these eight terms to talk about identity types. Some words may already be familiar to you, but they have a specialized usage for this topic.

extroverted   feeling   introverted   intuitive
judging   perceiving   sensing   thinking

1 **Complete the definitions of identity types with the words in the box.**

1 _____ people make decisions based on logical evidence.

2 People who draw conclusions based on their ideas and concepts of the world are known as _____.

3 People with a strong _____ identity are most comfortable with rules and specific guidelines. They see the world as an orderly place that always operates the same way.

4 _____ people are outgoing and sociable. They are interested in other people and the world around them.

5 _____ people use emotions and feelings to guide their choices.

6 People who focus on their own inner world are _____. They often prefer to spend time alone or without distractions from the outside.

7 If you are someone who thinks any situation can have many different outcomes, that there is no stable structure in place, and so anything is possible, you are probably a _____ person.

8 _____ people rely on concrete information; for example, evidence that can be seen, heard, or felt.

2 **The identity traits can be seen as four pairs of opposites. Match the traits (1–4) with their opposites (a–d).**

1 introverted

2 sensing

3 thinking

4 judging

a feeling

b extroverted

c perceiving

d intuitive

3 **Work in a group. Discuss the questions.**

1 Which identity traits do you think you have? Why do you think so?

2 It is possible to take free, online tests that will determine your identity type. Do you think such tests are useful and reliable? Why / why not?

Academic words

1 Match the words in bold with the correct definitions.

1 **comprehensive** (adj)	a result; consequence
2 **journal** (n)	b the extent or range of something
3 **outcome** (n)	c having all or nearly all parts or aspects of something
4 **scope** (n)	
5 **variables** (n pl)	d a person who participates in an activity without being paid
6 **volunteer** (n)	e a professional magazine that covers research about one topic
	f elements, features, or factors

2 Complete the paragraph with words from Exercise 1. Change the form if necessary.

This psychology [1]_____ has an interesting article about a very [2]_____ study carried out on a group of 500 [3]_____. The study tested whether people were honest about representing their identity online. The [4]_____ of the study was broad: it took into account such [5]_____ as age, gender, hours per week spent online, and years of online use. I was surprised by the [6]_____, which suggested that the majority of people exaggerated information about themselves, held information back, and in some cases, even posted information that wasn't true.

3 Work with a partner. Discuss the questions.

1 Do you think a study has to be comprehensive in order to be reliable? Is it possible to take all of the important variables into account?

2 If the outcome of a study doesn't have important implications, do you think it should still be published in a journal? Why / why not?

Critical thinking

Generalization

A danger when writing about identity traits is to assume people have traits that they might not, just because of a group they belong to. As you read, ask yourself if any generalizations are reasonable.

Professional basketball players are tall is reasonable.
People who play basketball are tall is not.

Some generalizations are more hidden. Consider the difference:
Boys who do well at sports are likely to develop social skills as well.
Children who do well at sports are likely to develop social skills as well.

The study that showed a person's personality can change over time was interesting to me. I can apply this to my own life in college. For example, I have often struggled with groupwork done outside of class. The people in the groups I'm in never seem to get along with one another. The hardest part of groupwork for me actually isn't the academic work, but choosing the people in my group. I don't want to work with a girl who talks too much or a guy who's too pushy and takes over the whole project. However, if it's true that personalities can change, then even someone who isn't a good group member could learn how to become one. This inspires me to study more about how to work with other people and how to teach them how to work well in groups.

1 Read the paragraph. Find the two over-generalizations. How could you reword them so that they are not over-generalizations?

2 Analyze the following statements. Check (✓) the ones that are valid.

☐ Every day more than 10,000 Americans retire from their jobs, which is putting an increasing strain on some social services.

☐ One problem with bringing more women into the workforce is that when they have babies, they typically abandon their jobs.

☐ Because shorter children have lower self-esteem, it's important for teachers to take this into account when considering forming study groups.

☐ Sports teams enjoy the "home advantage," meaning they play better in their own towns, in part because of the enthusiastic support of their fans.

3 Work with a partner. Discuss the questions.

1 What should you do when you read an over-generalization in a book? Or when you hear an over-generalization in a conversation?

2 Why do you think people make over-generalizations? Is this something you do? In what circumstances can they be useful or helpful?

Writing model

You are going to learn about using reflexive pronouns to show relationships between people, and practice different brainstorming techniques to gather ideas for a short essay about identity.

A Model

1   Read the essay prompt. Underline the key words.

   "*Some people believe that you are not born with a fixed identity and that how you are raised determines your personality. How far do you agree with this idea?*

   Give reasons for your answer and include any relevant examples from your own knowledge or experience."

2   Read the student model essay. Were all parts of the question answered?

> 1   The "nature or nurture" argument is a common one in the social sciences. Is a person born with their identity, or is it a result of the people around them, such as parents, teachers, and peers? Both research and personal experience have led me to think that the most important factor is the identity that people have from birth.
>
> 2   Comprehensive studies published in journals describe twins who grew up with the same parents, the same friends, and went to the same schools, and yet had very different personalities. The only reasonable explanation is that they had a different identity from birth, so the same outside influences had different effects on them. Similarly, children in the same class at school experience many of the same outside influences, but they are all very different from one another.
>
> 3   I have experienced this myself in my own family. My brother is only 15 months older than I am, but we have very different identities. He is a thinking, judging person. He needs to know all the facts and variables before making a decision. I rely on my feelings and intuition.
>
> 4   In conclusion, both the outcomes of studies and what I have observed in my own life have convinced me that nature is a stronger force than nurture.

B Analyze

1   Label paragraphs 1–4 with a purpose. Some labels are not used; a label may be used more than once.

   conclusion   implication   introduction   problem   solution   supporting example

2   Underline the thesis statement. Which paragraph does it appear in?

3   The writer gives an example from outside research and also a personal example. Which one appears first? Why, do you think?

Grammar

Reflexive pronouns

Use a reflexive pronoun (*myself, yourself, himself, herself, itself, ourselves, yourselves, themselves*) when the object of a sentence is the same person, thing, or idea as the subject:

Hiroshi sent Hiroshi a copy of the email.

~~Hiroshi sent him a copy of the email.~~ (This sounds like Hiroshi sent the email to another person.)

✓ Hiroshi sent <u>himself</u> a copy of the email.

Reflexive pronouns are sometimes used to add emphasis:

Jane criticized her employees for being late, yet she herself was frequently late. (she and *herself* are the same person—Jane.)

Reflexive pronouns frequently follow the preposition *by*:

You don't have to finish the project <u>by yourself</u>.

1 Complete the sentences with the correct reflexive pronoun.

  1 It is important that all the students do their work by _____.

  2 Send me a copy of the report, and also keep one for _____.

  3 When we looked at the old photo, we couldn't recognize _____.

  4 Dr. Kim's early research was directly related to his new study, so he quoted _____ in the journal article.

  5 Amina was able to finish the work _____, so she didn't ask for any help.

2 Rewrite the sentences with a reflexive pronoun to add emphasis.

  1 You are responsible for paying the fee.

  2 I don't believe identity is very important.

  3 Nobody was more surprised by the results of the study than the researchers!

  4 Ms. Jimenez couldn't believe the outcome of her research.

  5 Jack created the contest, and then he won it!

3 Work with a partner. Find the reflexive pronouns in *How permanent is your personality?* For each one, discuss which person or persons it refers to. Which one is used to add emphasis?

Writing skill

Before you write a longer text, such as an essay, you need to gather ideas
so you will have something to organize and then write about. This idea-
gathering is called *brainstorming*. Different methods of brainstorming suit
different writers and different essay topics. Learning to brainstorm quickly
will help you write better essays on timed exams.

1   Label the examples of brainstorming.

chart   free writing   word map

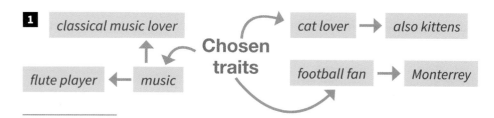

1

classical music lover   cat lover → also kittens

Chosen
traits

flute player ← music   football fan → Monterrey

_____

2

For me, I think my most important personality traits are my acheived
ones. I mean I can't help the ~~born ones~~ ones I was born with so I don't
really count those. ~~If I had been born taller, I could have been better at~~
~~sports, I think, so I regret that a little, but I don't think about it so much.~~
I focuss (sp??) more on what I can choice myself. When I ~~acheive~~ achieve
something through my own efforts, it means more to me because

_____

3 ascribed	achieved	chosen
short	honor student	flute player (or achieved?)
black hair	high school graduate	Monterrey football fan!!
Mexican	driver's license	cat lover

_____

2   Choose one of these topics. Brainstorm for five minutes using one of the methods
above. Then brainstorm for another five minutes using a different method.

•   An achieved personality trait I am proud of.

•   An identity trait I want to change.

•   A recent or new identity trait of mine.

3   Work with a partner. Which brainstorming method helped you get the most
ideas? Which one would be easiest for you to write an essay from?

Writing task

You are going to write a short essay in response to the following:
"Some people believe that your personality doesn't change over time. To what extent to do you agree with this idea? Give specific examples to support your opinion."

Brainstorm

Choose one of the brainstorming methods from page 23. Brainstorm for at least five minutes.

Plan

Look at your brainstorming notes. Decide your answer to the question. If you didn't write any specific examples, brainstorm again using the same method or a different one.

Write

Use your notes to help you write your essay. Remember to use reflexive pronouns where appropriate. Your text should be 250 words long.

Share

Exchange your essay with a partner. Use the checklist on page 189 and provide feedback to your partner.

Rewrite and edit

Consider your partner's comments and write your final draft. Think about:

- whether you answered the question clearly
- whether you used reflexive pronouns appropriately
- whether you had a clear introduction and conclusion.

Review

Wordlist

MACMILLAN
DICTIONARY

Vocabulary preview

confirm (v) ***	define (v) ***	participant (n) **
consequences (n) ***	desirable (adj) **	rate (v) **
correlation (n) *	frustrated (adj) *	suggest (v) ***
current (adj) ***	mature (v) *	tend (v) ***
debate (n) ***	modest (adj) **	tensions (n) ***

Vocabulary development

extroverted (adj)	intuitive (adj)	sensing (adj)
feeling (adj)	judging (adj)	thinking (adj) *
introverted (adj)	perceiving (adj)	

Academic words

comprehensive (adj) **	outcome (n) ***	variables (n) **
journal (n) **	scope (n) **	volunteer (n) **

Academic words review

Complete the sentences with the words in the box.

comprehensive	outcome	scope	variables	volunteer

1 A new study with a larger _____ is planned by psychologists.

2 As a _____, I was asked questions about my social identity.

3 Psychologists said the study was too limited and not _____ enough.

4 From the study's _____ we still have a lot to learn about personality types.

5 There are many different _____ that may have influenced the participants' answers.

Unit review

Reading 1	☐	I can recognize and understand classification texts.
Reading 2	☐	I can recognize substitution words.
Study skill	☐	I can develop self-awareness and self-evaluation skills.
Vocabulary	☐	I can use vocabulary to describe personality types.
Grammar	☐	I can use reflexive pronouns.
Writing	☐	I can use techniques for brainstorming.

Discussion point

Discuss with a partner.

1 Why is work done by hand slower than work done by machine?

   Machines can work faster because …

2 Are there any tasks that can be done faster by hand than by machine?

   One such task could be …

3 Are there any tasks that cannot be done by machine at all?

   I think / I don't think there are …

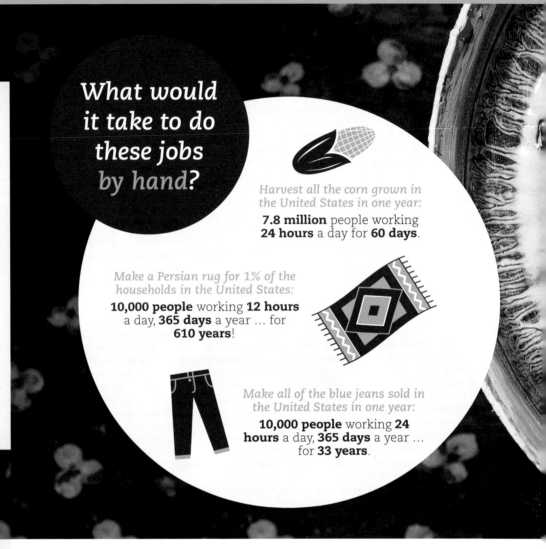

What would it take to do these jobs by hand?

Harvest all the corn grown in the United States in one year:

7.8 million people working **24 hours** a day for **60 days**.

Make a Persian rug for 1% of the households in the United States:

10,000 people working **12 hours** a day, **365 days** a year … for **610 years**!

Make all of the blue jeans sold in the United States in one year:

10,000 people working **24 hours** a day, **365 days** a year … for **33 years**.

VIDEO

MAN VERSUS MACHINE

Before you watch

Match the words in bold with the correct definitions.

1 **artisan** (n)   a a part of a situation

2 **decline** (v)   b a percentage of the money you earn that is paid to the government

3 **factor** (n)

4 **income tax** (n)   c a skilled person who makes things by hand

5 **pottery** (n)   d pots and dishes and other things that are made from clay

                       e to become smaller or fewer

UNIT AIMS

READING 1 Recognizing paraphrasing
READING 2 Recognizing examples
STUDY SKILL Writing a first draft

VOCABULARY Adjectives to describe products
GRAMMAR Using *can* to express universal truths
WRITING Organizing your brainstorm

Potter sculpting a vase.

While you watch

Read the sentences then watch the video. Write *T* (True), or *F* (False).

1 In the pottery industry in Tunisia there are too many cheap imports and high taxes. ____

2 The tax the potters have to pay is around 78 U.S. dollars a month. ____

3 They compete with the cheaper imports by exporting their own pottery at lower prices. ____

4 The artisans think the international importers and traders should help them. ____

After you watch

Discuss these questions with a partner.

1 Do you think the government should help these artisans?

   Yes, I do / No, I don't because …

2 What kinds of artisans do you have in your country? What do they produce?

   We have …   They produce …

3 Which do you prefer, modern or traditional designs?

   I prefer … because …

Beautifully broken

A Vocabulary preview

Match the words in bold with the correct definitions.

1   **flaw** (n)
2   **imitate** (v)
3   **incident** (n)
4   **modest** (adj)
5   **piece** (n)
6   **practice** (n)
7   **smash** (v)
8   **value** (v)

a   to break something with force, and into many pieces
b   a characteristic of not talking about your achievements or successes
c   to copy something; to do something in the same way
d   to consider something as important
e   a method or way of doing something
f   a complete artwork, such as a painting or sculpture
g   a mistake or imperfection
h   one event or occurrence

B Before you read

Preparing to read

Discuss these questions with a partner or group.

1   What do you usually do with dishes that break? Do you repair them or throw them away? Why?
2   Do you have any household objects that you have repaired? If so, why did you choose to keep them and repair them instead of replacing them?
3   What are some advantages and disadvantages to throwing away broken items?

C Global reading

Understanding organization

How is the reading organized? Scan the text, and then check (✓) your answer.

1   ☐   From past events to present events to future events
2   ☐   From definitions to examples to applications
3   ☐   From explanations to advantages to disadvantages
4   ☐   From definitions to comparisons to contrasts
5   ☐   From problems to solutions to advantages

Beautifully broken

1 Oh, no! You dropped the cup, and it smashed! Time to throw it away and buy a new one.

2 Unless, perhaps, you are a fan of the Japanese art of *kintsugi* or *kintsukuroi*—roughly translated, "to mend with gold." This is the practice among certain craftsmen of mending the broken pieces of pottery, such as a plate, cup, or a bowl,

Kintsugi bowl

with gold (or similar) lacquer. The gold is used to glue the pieces back together. If small pieces are missing, they can be created out of gold, or a piece from a different bowl or plate can be used instead. The repaired product's value is not reduced, though—it is actually enhanced. It is believed to become more beautiful because it was broken. Pieces of *kintsugi* pottery can be enormously expensive and are featured in museum exhibits in Japan and overseas.

3 These days you can even see machine-made ceramics with gold designs on them that look as if they are *kintsugi*, even though the original was actually never broken. But the mended patterns have become so trendy that people want to imitate them.

4 There's a story or legend behind the practice—which may or may not be historically accurate, but beautifully illustrates the concept. Back in the 1500s, there lived a military ruler in Japan, who owned a bowl he especially loved. One day while he was entertaining some guests, his servant dropped the bowl, and it broke into five pieces. Knowing the leader's bad temper, his guests worried that he would punish the servant. However, one of the guests made up an amusing poem about the incident. Everybody laughed, including the ruler. When he relaxed, he was able to see that the bowl's beauty had not been destroyed by the accident. Instead, because the vessel could be repaired, the ruler now had a new appreciation for its strength and ability to survive. In fact, according to the story, the true life of the bowl began the moment it was dropped.

5 If this seems a hard notion to understand, then consider it in light of another Japanese philosophy, that of *wabi-sabi*. This is harder to translate into English, but it refers to the combination of three beliefs: that nothing is permanent, nothing is finished, and nothing is perfect. Applied to arts and crafts, it explains why the Japanese traditionally value handmade objects. Even though they look less perfect than those made by machine, it is actually this imperfection that makes them beautiful. In fact, artists who value the *wabi-sabi* aesthetic create works that are deliberately imperfect, such as a bowl that isn't entirely round or a vase with a thumbprint visible in the clay. Rough surfaces, instead of ones smoothed by machines, are common in *wabi-sabi* ceramics, and often the pieces are not glazed or colored.

6 It's not just Japan that has such a tradition, however. A similar idea can be found in Iran, among the makers of Persian rugs. Tradition has it that those who weave carpets will deliberately include one small flaw, as recognition of the fact that nothing can be perfect. The intentional mistake reminds them to be modest about their work. Similarly, some early American settlers known as the Puritans included a "humility square" when they sewed a quilt—one square that didn't match the rest of the blanket. Some Native American bead workers would include an intentional "mistake bead" for the same reason.

7 Such practices have also been reported among Amish furniture makers in the United States and some forms of Islamic art—although careful work by sociologists and historians suggest that these stories are actually not true, but rather a romanticized version of their art or a misunderstanding of a tradition.

8 True or not, however, these cultural practices teach us not only about art but about life, and the importance of not only accepting, but actually celebrating, our imperfections. That doesn't mean we shouldn't care about making mistakes; but for many people, worrying about small imperfections keeps them from finishing a project or appreciating one they have finished. People who are "perfectionists" can feel insecure and anxious about the art they create, which makes it harder for them to enjoy what they do.

9 The concept can even be applied more broadly than just to art, however. Consider yourself, for example. Do you have any imperfections—anything from physical scars to personal habits? What if, instead of considering these to be flaws, you could appreciate them as part of what makes you a beautiful person?

"Wabi-sabi" bowl

That's easier said than done, but if you can understand and apply the concepts of *kintsugi* and *wabi-sabi* to your own life, you may be able to consider yourself with more kindness and humility, and to see yourself, flaws and all, as a true work of art.

GLOSSARY

aesthetic (n) the beauty of something; how it looks

humility (n) having a modest view of your own importance; being humble

D Close reading

Writers use paraphrasing to avoid repetition, which makes their texts more interesting and sophisticated. One way to do this is with a synonym:

*It's my family's **habit** to begin each dinner by talking about our day. We began this **custom** when I was in high school.*

Another way is to use a different word form:

*Jin Su **broke** the cup when she dropped it. However, she was able to repair the **break**, and so she could still use the broken cup.*

1 Read these sentence excerpts and find them in *Beautifully broken*. Then choose the correct synonym for the underlined word, according to the context. The first one is done for you.

1 This is the <u>practice</u> among certain craftsmen of mending the broken pieces of pottery.

   a art   b ritual   (c) habit

2 Knowing the <u>leader</u>'s bad temper …

   a president   b premier   c ruler

3 … because the <u>vessel</u> could be repaired …

   a bowl   b ship   c accident

4 The intentional <u>mistake</u> reminds them …

   a error   b flaw   c tradition

5 … one square that didn't match the rest of the <u>blanket</u>.

   a humility square   b quilt   c settlers

2 Read the text and the sentences. Write *T* (True), *F* (False), or *NG* (Not Given).

1 A dish that has been mended with the *kintsugi* technique will be more expensive than the original. ____

2 *Kintsugi* is an older tradition than carpet making in Iran. ____

3 A piece of art made in the *wabi-sabi* does not look handmade. ____

4 A humility square is a type of deliberate flaw. ____

5 If you deliberately make mistakes in your life, you will feel less anxious. ____

E Critical thinking

1 According to the article, the story about the Japanese ruler is probably not true nor are interpretations of some practices from other cultures. Should people still discuss those stories? Why / why not?

2 Do you believe it is ever possible for a work of art to be perfect?

Study skills Writing a first draft

Use your plan. Don't worry about style or good English at this stage.

Focus on the assignment question.

Clarify your core points. Write out your central ideas, hypotheses, conclusions, or the main direction of your line of reasoning.

Write headings and subheadings. Use your plan to identify these.

Add in supporting details below each heading.

Link it up. Write your headings and points into sentences.

Stick to your plan. Keep looking back to it after writing each paragraph. Go back to the assignment title and its central questions. Be a harsh critic of your own work.

© Stella Cottrell (2013)

1   Write the advice from the *Writing a first draft* box into the appropriate stage of the writing process.

Pre-writing / planning	Writing the first draft	Editing and revising

2   Read the following question. Write down your interpretation of the question and discuss it with a partner.

"Discuss some advantages of machine-made products over handmade products. Use specific reasons and examples in your answer."

3   Discuss the topic with a partner and think of the core points you would include in your answer.

4   Break down the main ideas into headings and subheadings, and make notes on each.

5   Compare your ideas with a partner. Would your essays have a similar structure?

Community development: A new business in town

A Vocabulary preview

1 Match the words and phrases in bold with the correct definitions.

1	**delicate** (adj)	a	useful; practical; not decorative
2	**entirely** (adv)	b	friendly to; getting along well with
3	**functional** (adj)	c	lightweight or fragile; easily broken
4	**harm** (v)	d	heavy; the opposite of thin
5	**objection** (n)	e	an idealistic impression
6	**on good terms with** (phrase)	f	an expression of disagreement or disapproval
7	**romantic** (adj)	g	completely; totally
8	**thick** (adj)	h	to damage, injure, or hurt something or someone

2 Complete the sentences with words and phrases from Exercise 1. Change the form if necessary.

1 I'm not _____ my neighbors. We have a lot of disagreements.

2 Those boots are not made _____ of leather. The bottoms are made of rubber.

3 My parents can't judge their old home realistically. They have a _____ impression of it, and think it's better than it really was.

4 Don't put hot dishes directly on the table. You might _____ the wood.

5 If you don't have any _____, I'm going to buy this chair.

6 Wool sweaters can be very _____, so they're warm in winter.

7 This chair isn't very attractive, but it's _____, so I keep it.

8 Be careful with those glasses! They're very _____ and break easily.

B Before you read

Preparing to read

You will read an interview between a community reporter and a representative for a company that is building a large factory there. What questions might the reporter ask? What information might the representative offer?

C Global reading

Reading for tone

1 Skim the article. Do the two people mostly agree or mostly disagree?

2 Is the tone of the interview friendly? How can you tell?

COMMUNITY DEVELOPMENT:
A NEW BUSINESS IN TOWN

In this month's community development column, our reporter Karen Brandt talks with Julian Vincenzo, the public relations officer for Mayflower Quality Home Furnishings.

Karen Brandt: Thank you for agreeing to talk with me, Julian. And welcome to the city of Carrollton.

Julian Vincenzo: It's my pleasure, Karen. We at Mayflower think it's essential to be on good terms with the Carrollton community, and for that reason, I'm very appreciative of this opportunity to talk to you about our company and what we do, and what we have to offer.

KB: First of all, let me just say, you're very brave to choose a city like this one to locate your new factory in.

JV: Well, I'm not sure *brave* is how I'd interpret it … we looked at quite a few cities around the state, and chose this one because it offered the perfect location for what we need. That is, sufficient land and enough workers.

KB: Yes, I understand that. I'm referring though to, well, some of the objections you've faced from residents here. For instance, from people who say that your company philosophy is the opposite of the Carrollton spirit. This is a very old community, as you know, and its residents have been famous for one thing for a considerable time—hundreds of years, actually.

JV: I'm glad you brought that up, Karen, because I'd like to talk about that. I appreciate that Carrollton has been known for generations for handmade furniture. In fact, my grandparents have some old Carrollton pieces, like a writing desk and a table and a set of chairs, and they're beautiful. I sincerely respect that craftsmanship and tradition.

KB: And yet Mayflower is a company that produces furniture entirely by machine. Your factory is going to be manufacturing the same kinds of furniture that craftspeople here have been making, except not with people—with robots and equipment. You can see why people are concerned that this might harm the handcrafted furniture traditions here.

JV: I can understand the worry, but I think people need to take the many advantages of machine-made furniture into consideration.

KB: Such as?

JV: Well, as one example, affordability. Because machines can produce furniture faster and more cheaply, the prices are lower. That means the finished product, the furniture, is available to more people. A hand-carved rocking chair might be beautiful, but if someone doesn't have enough money to buy it, then they're not going to enjoy it. If you agree with me—and I assume you do—that furniture is practical as well as beautiful, then you can see why we feel it needs to be affordable, so ordinary people can purchase it.

KB: That's a good point, I'll admit. I know the handmade pieces can be expensive. But they're high quality, so they last a long time. Like the example you gave of your grandparents' furniture.

JV: But remember that machine-made doesn't mean low quality. Quite the opposite. Machines are actually better at some tasks than people. One example is working with weight, with heavy things—like wood. A machine can lift a plank of wood that weighs several hundred pounds and hold it perfectly still. A person just can't do that. Let me ask you—do any of the furniture makers here ever have physical problems because of how heavy their work is? For instance, sore shoulders or bad backs?

KB: Yes, sometimes. Of course, there are techniques that workers use to prevent injuries, but they're not always entirely successful.

JV: Another example is with very delicate work. Machines don't face some of the challenges that people do, such as hands that shake or thick fingers. A machine doesn't get cold or nervous or sleepy and make a mistake. Wood isn't like paper—you can't erase a mistake. If you damage a piece of wood, you often have to replace it and start again.

KB: Well, I know. I can't argue with that. It does take time and a lot of patience to do the really delicate work.

JV: I'm glad you mentioned time, Karen, because that's another example of an advantage of the machine-made process—it's just faster.

KB: I agree, but does that really matter? The stores here are full of finished pieces. A customer doesn't usually have to wait for a chair to be made.

JV: Not an individual chair, necessarily, but think of how fast trends change. A machine can keep up with that faster than a human. That desk my grandparents have is beautiful, but it's not very practical for handling all the cords and power strips that today's computers and electronics require, for instance. People are constantly updating the look of their living rooms, their kitchens, their offices, and machines can keep up with that.

KB: Oh, I know. Maybe it's just that I have a romantic notion of handcrafted furniture. It's so beautiful, and so … well, so human. I think that means something. Do you see my point?

JV: I do, and I don't disagree. But remember—machines were made by humans. People designed our machines so well that they're able to create beautiful, functional furniture. The artistry of the furniture still comes from people. It's only the work that has been automated.

KB: I understand what you're saying, although I think people here would argue that the work itself, the actual cutting and carving of the wood, is important. Don't you worry about the people who do that who will lose their jobs?

JV: Well, I think there will always be a market for handcrafted works of art, including furniture. All we're doing is bringing affordable furniture to many more people. And rather than taking jobs away, we're bringing more jobs to Carrollton. Our factory will employ people in all kinds of jobs, such as sales and marketing, telephone support, and shipping, to name just a few. It's not the same kind of work, I know, but motivated people can always learn new skills.

KB: Julian, thank you so much for taking the time to talk with me, and to explain what Mayflower can bring to Carrollton.

JV: My pleasure, Karen. And I hope to see you in our showroom sometime!

GLOSSARY

affordable (adj) cheap enough for ordinary people to afford

automated (adj) using machines or done by machines, instead of people

D Close reading

Giving examples is a common way to explain points or to offer support for an opinion or argument. Examples can be as short as one word or as long as a story. Here are some common ways in which authors signal examples:

As one / another example,

That is,

To illustrate (this),

Namely,

One / Another example is …

such as / like

to name just a few

Writers don't always use these signal phrases for examples. However, when you see them in the text, you will know that the example is particularly important.

Match the examples from the reading with the idea they are supporting or explaining. Then write the word or phrase that the author used to signal the example.

1   There are sufficient workers and land
2   Affordability
3   Working with heavy things
4   Speed
5   Sales and marketing

a   Something machines are better at than people
b   Jobs that the new factory will bring
c   An advantage of the machine-made process
d   An advantage of machine-made furniture
e   Why Carrollton is a good location for the new factory

E Critical thinking

Work in a group. Discuss the questions.

1   The reporter began her questions from a biased point of view. What was her bias? Do you think she changed her mind during the interview?
2   What do you think is the most important benefit that Mayflower could bring to Carrollton? What is the biggest harm it might do?
3   What do you imagine Ms. Brandt and Mr. Vincenzo would think about the concept of *wabi-sabi?* Why?

Vocabulary development

Adjectives for describing products

1 Write the words in the box into the correct categories. Then discuss your choices with a partner. If you made any different choices, discuss why.

appealing   contemporary   durable   fake   generic
innovative   mass-produced   multifunctional

Positive	Negative	Neutral

2 Write an example of each type of product that you own or have seen. Then share your answers with a partner.

1 Something you're wearing that was mass-produced:

_____

2 Something in your home that is multifunctional:

_____

3 Something in the room you are in now that's durable:

_____

4 Something you bought in the last year that's versatile:

_____

5 Something you've seen that is fake:

_____

6 Something you like that is generic:

_____

7 Something in your school that is contemporary:

_____

8 Something you wish to buy that is innovative:

_____

Academic words

1 Match the words in bold with the correct definitions.

1 **enhance** (v)
2 **notion** (n)
3 **overseas** (adv)
4 **philosophy** (n)
5 **survive** (v)
6 **tradition** (n)

a to live, endure, or continue, especially in the face of a threat or difficulty
b a way of thinking; a belief or attitude in life
c to make something better by adding to it
d in another country
e an activity or custom that has continued over time
f idea; concept

2 Complete the sentences with words from Exercise 1. Change the form if necessary.

1 Fortunately, the pottery and sculptures in the museum _____ the earthquake.

2 The _____ that handmade items are more special is not one that everyone agrees with.

3 My personal _____ is that design should always be functional.

4 Indonesia has a _____ of making *Batik*—a way of dying fabric.

5 The furniture maker _____ the chair by carving birds and flowers into the back of it.

6 Some people travel _____ to find special handcrafted items.

3 Work in a group. Discuss the questions using vocabulary from Exercise 1.

1 Think of some of the things that you own. Do you think their value will increase or decrease over time? Why? How long do you think they will survive?

2 Is there a particular artistic tradition in your country? Do you think it is important to protect and maintain such traditions?

Critical thinking

Flawed arguments

When a writer presents an argument, it is important to always assess the strength of their reasoning. Sometimes arguments can appear convincing, but on closer examination they lack the evidence needed to persuade the reader.

Some common examples of flawed arguments are:

- repeatedly restating the claim, without providing supporting evidence
- attacking the opposing view, rather than supporting your own
- using irrelevant evidence, which may be interesting, but does not support the argument.

1 Read the following texts and match a type of flawed argument to each one.

Attacking the opposing view   Repeatedly restating the claim
Using irrelevant evidence

1 Handmade products are far more important to our culture than manufactured products because they have a link to our past and our ancestors. This is why handmade products are so vital to our culture and more valuable than those products made in a factory. These kinds of products made by hand are so important we have to make sure we keep making them to protect our culture in the long term.

2 In my opinion manufactured goods are far preferable to those made by hand. Handmade products are expensive and time-consuming to produce and quality can vary enormously from product to product. This is why you could not make a computer or mobile phone by hand. The parts would cost too much and quality issues would make these devices unreliable. This is why manufactured products are better.

3 Making products by hand is extremely important. For example, in my country many people like to use handmade tea cups for tea ceremonies. Tea ceremonies are an ancient tradition dating back hundreds of years. We use powdered green tea and a number of other objects to enjoy a tea ceremony. They can be held indoors or outdoors and there are two main seasons for them; tea ceremonies in the warmer months and in the months of winter.

2 Work with a partner. Choose one of the texts and discuss ways to improve it.

Writing model

You are going to learn about using *can* to express general truths and how to organize and edit your ideas. You are then going to use these skills to write an essay expressing advantages and disadvantages.

A Model

1 Read the essay prompt. Underline the key words that tell what must be included in the answer.

"Discuss some advantages of machine-made products over handmade products. Use specific reasons and examples in your answer."

2 Read the student model. How many advantages did the writer discuss? Which was the most important one, do you think?

People can often have romantic notions of the value of handmade items. They might even consider handmade items to be better than those made by machine. While it's true that handmade pieces can be very beautiful, there are three important advantages to machine-made items.

First, machine-made items are inexpensive. This means that more people can afford to buy them, and that everyone who buys them can save money. For example, in my town, there is a shop that sells handmade shirts and dresses. One shirt can cost $200 or more. A shirt that looks almost exactly the same in a store, however, can cost $50, or even less if it is on sale.

Another important reason is that machine-made items are high quality. Machines do not make mistakes like people do, so products usually do not have flaws or imperfections such as rough surfaces or broken pieces.

Finally, machines can make many products that are identical, such as chairs that are all the same size and shape, or pianos that are all of the same quality. This means that many different people can enjoy the same product in the same way. People have an equal opportunity to own a product if there are many of them that are the same. This is both useful and fair.

Even if we like to watch one master woodcarver creating a unique product, we should remember that it is machines that can produce pieces that are affordable, safe, durable, and available to everybody.

B Analyze

1 Which sentence is the thesis statement? How many sentences come before the thesis statement, and what is their purpose?

2 How did the writer signal the reasons and examples? Underline the phrases.

3 The writer mentioned handmade products a few times. Why?

Grammar

Using *can* for universal truths

Can is used to talk about things that are often true or that are possible. (*Be able to* cannot be used as a synonym for *can* in this sense.)

*Handmade items **can** be very beautiful.*

Writers often **hedge** their use of *can* with adverbs such as *sometimes*, *often*, and *usually*, and phrases such as *in some cases*, *in some circumstances*, and *in some situations*. This shows that the situation is not necessarily always true.

*Handmade items **can** sometimes be very expensive.*

*Handmade items **can** be very expensive in some cases.*

*In some cases, handmade items **can** be very expensive.*

1 Reorder the words to make sentences.

  1 very / it / sew a quilt/ take a / long / can / time to

    It _____

  2 tell if / machine or / it can / difficult to/ a scarf / be / was / by hand / knitted by

    It _____

  3 well as / found in / people's homes as / can / works of art / in museums / usually be

    Works _____

  4 be understood through / the culture of / can often / its traditions / a country

    The _____

  5 a piece of / identify / at it / the maker of / some people can / just by looking / furniture

    Some _____

  6 art / many / perfect / craftsmen / believe that no / piece of / can be

    Many _____

2 Rewrite the sentences with *can* to express a universal truth. The first one has been done for you.

  1 It is relaxing to create art by hand. *It can be relaxing to create art by hand.*

  2 People are sometimes reluctant to pay more for imperfect items.

  3 Machinery is used to create things more quickly.

  4 Factories are located in both cities and small towns.

  5 Quilts are made by machine as well as by hand.

  6 People usually understand why handmade items cost more.

Writing skill

After you've brainstormed ideas for your paper, it's important to organize them. This step includes:

- deleting ideas you don't want to use
- adding ideas you didn't think of before
- choosing an order for your ideas

Typically, when you have two or more supporting examples or arguments, put the strongest or most convincing one last, where your reader will remember it best.

When you have selected which ideas to use for your body paragraphs, write a topic sentence for each one. If you are taking a timed essay exam, write your outline onto the paper or screen, and then fill it in with the time remaining. If you run out of time, you may still get credit for organization (which you would not otherwise).

1   Work with a partner. Discuss why the writer crossed out some ideas.

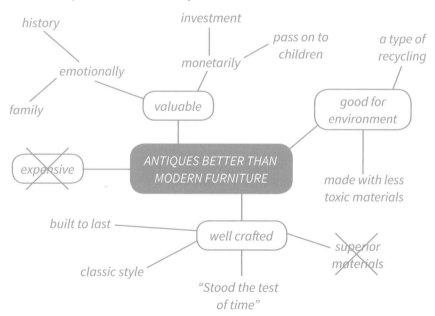

2   Read the brainstorm again. Number the supporting points from 1 (least interesting or important) to 3 (most interesting or important). Discuss your decisions with a partner. Did you agree?

3   Write a topic sentence for each supporting point. Then share your sentences with a partner or group.

Writing task

You are going to write an essay in response to the following:

"Discuss some advantages of handmade products over machine-made products. Use specific reasons and examples in your answer."

Brainstorm

Complete the brainstorm with your own ideas.

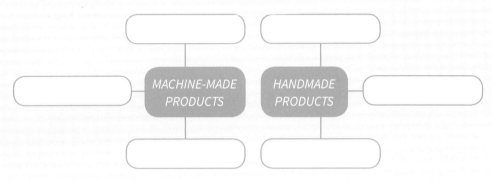

Plan

Look at your brainstorming notes. Write your thesis statement. Then cross out any ideas that don't support your thesis or that you don't want to use.

Write

Use your brainstorm to help you write your essay. Remember to use *can* to express general truths where appropriate. Your text should be 250 words long.

Share

Exchange your essay with a partner. Use the checklist on page 189 to help you provide feedback to your partner.

Rewrite and edit

Consider your partner's comments and write your final draft. Think about:

- whether you answered the question clearly
- whether you used *can* to express general truths appropriately
- whether you had a clear introduction and conclusion.

Review

Wordlist

MACMILLAN DICTIONARY

Vocabulary preview

delicate (adj) **	incident (n) ***	romantic (adj) **
entirely (adv) ***	modest (adj) **	smash (v) **
functional (adj) **	objection (n) **	thick (adj) ***
harm (v) *	piece (n) ***	value (v) **
imitate (v) *	practice (n) ***	

Vocabulary development

appealing (adj) *	generic (adj) *	mass-produced (adj)
contemporary (adj) ***	fake (adj)	multifunctional (adj)
durable (adj)	innovative (adj) *	

Academic words

enhance (v) **	overseas (adv)	survive (v) ***
notion (n) ***	philosophy (n) ***	tradition (n) ***

Academic words review

Complete the sentences with the words in the box.

enhance   journal   philosophy   survive   tradition

1   Some of the oldest practices have shown an impressive ability to
   _____.

2   Some believe that an object's imperfections can actually _____ its
   beauty.

3   I first learned about *wabi-sabi* in a _____ on Japanese culture.

4   Our company _____ is to use the finest materials possible.

5   Quilt making is an important _____ in my community.

Unit review

Reading 1	☐ I can recognize paraphrases.
Reading 2	☐ I can recognize examples.
Study skill	☐ I can write a draft essay.
Vocabulary	☐ I can use adjectives to describe products.
Grammar	☐ I can use *can* to express universal truths.
Writing	☐ I can organize my brainstorm.

Discussion point

Discuss with a partner.

1 Give some examples of things you have already done today that were controlled by different parts of the brain.

I cooked breakfast, so the cerebellum controlled my arms while I was cooking. Then …

2 Do you think your right-brain hemisphere or your left-brain hemisphere is more dominant? Why do you think so?

I think I'm more right-brained, because I love music and art, but I'm not so good at math.

The brain's control centre

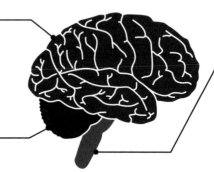

Cerebrum: controls the five senses, thinking, and emotions

Brainstem: controls automatic body functions such as breathing, heart rate, and digestion

Cerebellum: controls muscle movements

The Cerebrum

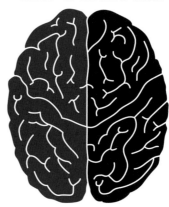

Left hemisphere: controls **speech, writing, comprehension,** and **math**

Right hemisphere: controls **emotions, creativity,** and **the arts**

VIDEO

VIRTUAL REALITY TREATMENT

Before you watch

Match the words in bold with the correct definitions.

1 **compassion** (n)
2 **psychologist** (n)
3 **treatment** (n)
4 **virtual reality** (n)

a a computer-generated environment that is similar to a real environment
b a feeling of concern and sympathy for others
c medical care given to a patient
d someone who studies the human mind

UNIT AIMS

READING 1 Understanding ellipsis
READING 2 The function of questions
STUDY SKILL Improving memory–association and mnemonics

VOCABULARY Language for comparing and contrasting
GRAMMAR Language for hedging
WRITING Organizing a comparison–contrast essay

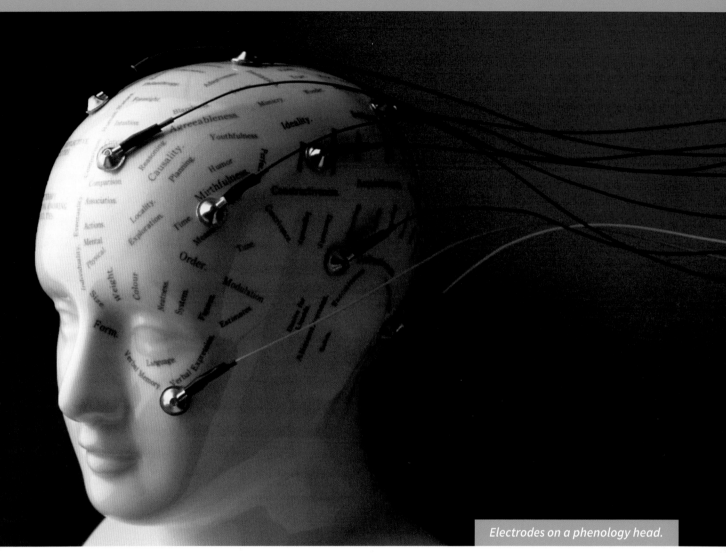

Electrodes on a phenology head.

While you watch

Watch the video and choose the correct option for each sentence.

1 When you wear the virtual reality suit, **cameras track your movements / you cry like a child**.

2 You see yourself **becoming / comforting** a child.

3 Studies show that increased self-compassion can **help prevent / cause** mental health problems.

4 The virtual reality suit could enable people to **get their treatment at home / play more video games at home**.

After you watch

Work with a partner. Discuss the questions.

1 Why do you think virtual reality treatment works?
   I think it works because …

2 Would you like to try the treatment?

3 Have you ever tried virtual reality?

4 Would you like to learn English using virtual reality?
   Yes, I think I would because …
   No, I wouldn't because …

The development of thought

A Vocabulary preview

Complete the sentences with the words in the box. Change the form if necessary.

concrete   constantly   fascination   hypothesize
lead to   logical   point of view   sort

1 Your brain _____ makes decisions based on what's happening around you.

2 Can you help me _____ this pile of papers into white and colored, so I can recycle them?

3 I have a _____ with the subject of psychology. It's so interesting!

4 He approached the problem in a very _____ way.

5 From his _____ there wasn't any need for further studies. The rest of the committee, however, had the opposite opinion.

6 After planning for several months, the committee finally came up with a _____ proposal.

7 Often one negative thought can _____ another.

8 When scientists can't identify a cause for something, they start by _____ and then check their guesses.

B Before you read

Making predictions

Work with a partner. Discuss the questions.

At what age do you think most children

• understand that when they can't see an object, it still exists?

• learn through playing?

• begin to think more about the feelings of other people?

C Global reading

Scanning

1 **Scan *The development of thought* to learn who these people are:**

Jean Piaget: _____

Jacqueline: _____

Gerard: _____

2 **Now read the article carefully. Check your predictions from *B Before you read*.**

The development of thought

1 Our bodies grow and develop as we age, so it should come as no surprise that our thoughts do too. Understanding the development of thought can help us understand our interactions with people of different ages, especially children and young adults.

2 The pioneer of the study of cognitive development is Jean Piaget (1896–1980), a French psychologist. Piaget formed his theories by both observing and talking to children, including his own, and by setting conventional intelligence tests. Piaget's method was innovative because rather than observing his subjects in a laboratory, he observed them in a natural setting, such as at play or in their homes.

3 Piaget's fascination with this subject grew from watching his nephew Gerard playing with a ball. He noted that when the ball rolled away from Gerard, but was still in sight, such as under a table, the child was able to find it and pick it up. However, when the ball rolled under a sofa, and Gerard could no longer see it, he tried to find it in the place he had seen it last. From this, Piaget hypothesized that young children lacked the ability to see objects as separate from themselves.

4 To test this, Piaget began carefully observing his own baby daughter, Jacqueline, as she grew up. As a baby, she apparently believed that objects did not exist if she could not see them. At nearly 12 months of age, she would search for missing objects she could no longer see—thus indicating that she knew they still existed. However, like Gerard in the prior example, she sometimes looked in the wrong place. At around 21 months, she seemed to clearly understand that objects existed whether she was looking at them or not.

5 Piaget concluded that adults not only think faster than children, but differently. Eventually, he categorized cognitive development into four stages:

THE SENSORIMOTOR STAGE (from birth to two years old): Infants and toddlers use input from their senses—seeing, touching, smelling, tasting, hearing—to understand their world. That's one reason toddlers are constantly putting non-edible objects into their mouths. They're not trying to eat; they're trying to learn. A principle goal of this stage is for children to learn "object permanence"; that is, to understand that an object exists even when they can't see it. This leads to their being able to name objects with words.

THE PREOPERATIONAL STAGE (from two to six years old): Children use play as a method of learning. They are *egocentric*, meaning that they have trouble understanding the point of view of other people, and are not good at logical thinking. Children have a more mature use of language than infants and toddlers, and can use symbols, memory, and imagination.

THE CONCRETE OPERATIONAL STAGE (from six or seven to 11 years old): Children have improved use of logic, and can reason mathematically. They can divide and sort items into categories, and think about two dimensions, such as length and width, at the same time. However, their logic applies mostly to concrete objects and not abstract or hypothetical ideas. At this stage, they become less egocentric and begin to consider the viewpoint and feelings of other people.

THE FORMAL OPERATIONAL STAGE (from age 11 or 12 on up): Adolescents can think logically about abstract and hypothetical ideas, such as what might happen in the future. They can understand complex mathematical formulas, and relationships such as cause and effect. At the beginning of this stage, there is a return to egocentric thought. It is estimated that only about 35% of high school graduates in industrialized countries reach this stage, and that many adults, in fact, never do.

6 Modern child psychologists have made adjustments to Piaget's theories. For example, it is now accepted that the ages of the four stages are approximate, and that there is some variation in the rate of children's development. However, the stages and their characteristics are still accepted and studied today.

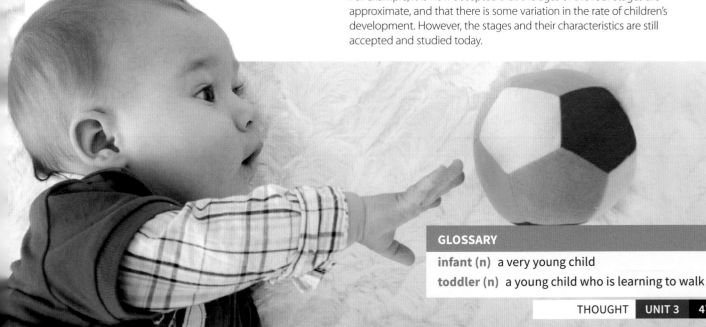

GLOSSARY

infant (n) a very young child

toddler (n) a young child who is learning to walk

D Close reading

Writers use ellipsis to eliminate unnecessary words. This can be done in one sentence:

Children learn about the world around them by using their senses, and adults do too. (Instead of writing, *adults learn about the world around them by using their senses too.*)

Ellipsis can also refer back to a previous sentence.

My father and mother didn't take many photographs of me when I was a baby. Neither even owned a camera. (Instead of, *Neither my father nor my mother.*)

Common words and phrases used for ellipsis include *so, too, neither, the former, the latter*, and forms of auxiliary verbs such as *do*, *have*, and *be*.

If you find ellipsis difficult while reading, remember to check back a few sentences.

Reread these sentences from *The development of thought*. Choose what the underlined ellipsis is referring to.

1 Our bodies grow and develop as we age, so it should come as no surprise that our thoughts <u>do</u> too—that is, the very way in which we think.

   a   age   b   think   c   grow and develop

2 Piaget formed his theories by both by observing and talking to children, including his <u>own</u>, and by setting conventional intelligence tests.

   a   children   b   theories   c   field

3 At the beginning of this stage, there is a return to egocentric thought. It is estimated that only about 35% of high school graduates in industrialized countries reach this stage, and that many adults, in fact, never <u>do</u>.

   a   think logically

   b   return to egocentric thought   c   reach this stage

E Critical thinking

Work in a group. Discuss the questions.

1 How can an understanding of the stages of the development of thought be useful to …

   parents?   teachers?   other adults?

2 According to the article, many adults never reach the formal operational stage. What do you think might be some reasons for this? Do you think it's important?

Study skills | Improving memory–association and mnemonics

To help you remember information you read, associate it with something else. For example, make notes about information in a text that reminds you of another reading or something else. Another technique is to create a mnemonic—a word formed from the first letter of other words. For example, to remember the names of the Great Lakes in the United States, people remember the word HOMES: **H**uron, **O**ntario, **M**ichigan, **E**rie, **S**uperior. You can also make sentence mneuomonics to help you remember how to spell words, for example, RHYTHM: **R**hythm **H**elps **Y**our **T**wo **H**ips **M**ove.

© Stella Cottrell (2013)

1 Match the mnemonic (1–6) with the information it is designed to help you remember (a–f).

1 King Henry Died Drinking Chocolate Milk

2 Riding On Your Grandmother's Bike Is Vile

3 Every Good Boy Deserves Fruit

4 Please Excuse My Dear Aunt Sally

5 My Very Educated Mother Just Served Us Nachos

6 FANBOYS

a The order of colors in the rainbow (red, orange, yellow, green, blue, indigo, violet)

b Planets in the solar system (Mercury, Venus, Earth, Mars, Jupiter, Saturn, Uranus, Neptune)

c Lines of the musical staff (E, G, B, D, F)

d Common metric system prefixes, in descending order of size (kilo-, hecto-, deca-, deci-, centi-, milli-)

e The coordinating conjunctions (for, and, nor, but, or, yet, so)

f Order of operations of mathematics (parentheses; exponents; multiplication and division; addition and subtraction)

2 Create a mnemonic to help you remember the stages of thought development. Then share your mnemonic with a partner or group. Can other people figure out how your mnemonic works?

Emotional thinking

A Vocabulary preview

1 Match the words in bold with the correct definitions.

1 **anxiety** (n)
2 **deadline** (n)
3 **emotions** (n)
4 **encounter** (v)
5 **guilt** (n)
6 **inappropriate** (adj)
7 **rational** (adj)
8 **strengthen** (v)

a the feeling you experience when you are worried about something
b to meet someone or something unexpectedly
c a time by which something has to be done or finished
d a strong feeling that you have done something wrong; a feeling of shame
e strong feelings
f not suitable; not proper
g based on reasons and facts
h to make something stronger

2 Complete the sentences with words from Exercise 1. Change the form if necessary.

1 I often feel _____ before an important presentation.

2 Please don't wear shorts to the office. It's _____ for business.

3 When you feel angry, it's difficult to make a _____ decision.

4 It's important to stay calm when you _____ problems at work.

5 Many interviews now include questions that test candidates' _____ intelligence.

6 It takes great _____ not to take some criticisms personally.

7 There's no need to feel _____. It wasn't your fault.

8 Some people do their best work when faced with tight _____.

B Before you read

Preparing to read

Work in a group. Discuss the questions.

1 Do you make decisions more from your head or from your heart?

2 Do you trust your "gut feelings"? That is, your instincts? Have you ever had a gut feeling that turned out to be right? How about one that was wrong?

C Global reading

Identifying text type

Read *Emotional thinking* and answer the questions.

1 Who is the audience for this text, and what is the tone?

2 What does the writer use bullets (•) to show? And why?

Emotional *thinking*

1 **Is it better to think with your head or your heart? The real question may be—do you have a choice? Even people who pride themselves on being logical, rational thinkers may be more influenced by their emotions than they realize.**

2 The reason for that is simple: Emotions are designed to influence behavior. Emotions evaluate a situation and then tell us how to react. When your brain experiences an emotion, it sends a signal to your nervous system, which in turn sends signals to the rest of your body. This is why people refer to a "gut feeling." Emotions give you this type of information more quickly and with a stronger impact than using your reasoning. They're designed to help you make decisions quickly, especially in "high stakes" situations, those that are very important or carry some element of risk.

3 Emotional responses are often built on past experiences. Have you ever had an unpleasant experience with a bully in school, for example? If you later encounter someone in a business meeting who reminds you of that person, perhaps because he looks similar or exhibits some of the same behavior, you might feel the same emotions you felt as a child, such as fear and anxiety, and be reluctant to interact with that person.

4 Popular articles encourage people to "Listen to your gut" and to "Trust your instincts." The problem is that these emotions won't always be correct. The person in the business meeting might not be a bully at all, but only share the same hair and eye color or tone of voice. Even though your emotions are telling you the two people are similar, it might not be true.

5 Emotional thinking has an important impact on the workplace because it influences how people decide what to do. Researchers have found that emotions carry out four key functions in decision-making:

- They provide information. Emotions tell you whether an experience or encounter is likely to be positive or negative. Pleasure and displeasure are two emotions that serve this function.

- They improve speed. Because emotions are felt more immediately than logical thought, they result in decisions being made faster. Fear, anger, and hunger are good examples of emotions that produce a rapid response.

- They assess relevance. Emotions such as regret and disappointment that are based on someone's personal history will influence how that person evaluates an event in the present.

- They strengthen commitment to others. Community and personal connection are important in social groups, and emotions such as guilt, love, and empathy guide people to help others in their group.

6 All of these functions are important on the job; but how good are emotions at carrying them out?

7 Studies conducted about the implication of emotional thinking in the workplace have found some interesting—and sobering—results. For example, when people feel angry, they are more likely to assume a situation is less risky than it really is, and also to be less willing to admit they have made a mistake. An angry manager might continue to support a failing project because he doesn't want to admit that he was wrong.

8 When people experience fear, on the other hand, they tend to give up on projects too easily. While anger gives people too much confidence, fear takes too much confidence away.

People feeling sad or depressed were found to be more likely to set low prices for items they were asked to sell. However, they were also more generous towards others.

9 People who feel happy are less likely to take risks. But even happiness is not all good news. More than one study has found that happy people put more emphasis on the appearance of something than quality. There's a reason why job interviews, when both people laugh and feel relaxed, are more likely to result in the candidate being offered the job.

10 If even positive feelings can lead to inappropriate decisions, what should a person do? While emotional thinking is inevitable, steps can be taken to add rational thinking as well. As emotional thoughts come more quickly, and yet might not be accurate, build extra time into your decision-making process. Give yourself enough time and opportunity to logically evaluate the situation. You can also force your brain to react impartially, for example, by making a list of advantages and disadvantages of a decision.

11 Understanding emotional thinking will help you better understand the way other people behave. If you can tell who is approaching a task with anger or fear, you will be better able to predict how they will act.

12 Nonetheless, the same event or circumstance can cause different emotions in different people. Almost everyone, for instance, feels anxiety or stress while working on projects with a deadline. But for some people, that anxiety begins as soon as the project is assigned. Other people only feel anxious when the deadline is very close. The first person will start working right away, in order to get rid of or lessen the sense of anxiety. But the second won't begin until the deadline is near because the anxiety hasn't been triggered yet. For managers, knowing which type of person each of their employees is will help with time management and choosing which people could work together on a team.

GLOSSARY

response (n) a reaction
risky (adj) involving the possibility of danger, harm, or failure

13 Ideally, you will never have to choose between emotional thinking and rational thinking. To maximize your ability to make good decisions, use both. Give your brain time to interpret the signals your emotions are giving you instead of relying solely on one type of input. Use every resource your body provides, in other words, instead of just some. It's the logical thing to do, and it feels right too.

D Close reading

Questions in a reading text can fulfil a number of different functions.

- **Interest:** Asking a question makes readers interested. They want to know the answer, so they read further. Sometimes a question is asked directly to the reader; this is common in introductions, for instance. The reader answers the question in his or her head, and then feels a connection to the subject.

- **Importance:** Some questions will be directly answered in the text, and it's important for the reader to learn the answer. A question then signals to the reader that this is essential information. If you see a question such as "What are the four stages of culture shock?" then you know it's important that you learn the four stages. Headings are sometimes phrased as questions for this purpose and exam tasks often refer to questions in reading texts.

1 Read *Emotional thinking* again. What is the purpose of these questions? Write *Interest* or *Importance*.

1 Is it better to think with your head or your heart? _____

2 The real question may be—do you have a choice? _____

3 Have you ever had an unpleasant experience with a bully in school, for example? _____

4 All of these functions are important on the job; but how good are emotions at carrying them out? _____

5 If even positive feelings can lead to inappropriate decisions, what should a person do? _____

2 For the questions in Exercise 1 that you marked as *Importance*, write the answers to the questions or discuss them with a partner.

E Critical thinking

Work in a group. Discuss the questions.

1 What are some reasons that people might have evolved to make emotional decisions more quickly than intellectual decisions?

2 What are some examples of decisions that should be made mostly emotionally, mostly intellectually, or equally emotionally and intellectually?

Vocabulary development

Language for comparing and contrasting

1   Categorize the words in the box into the chart.

> by the same token   despite   equally   in spite of
> in the same way   on the contrary   similarly   whereas

Words and phrases that compare	Words and phrases that contrast

2   Choose the correct word or phrase to complete the sentences.

1   I'm a very left-brained person. My brother, **in the same way / on the contrary**, is more right-brained.

2   **Despite / Whereas** everything we know about the brain, there is still a lot to discover.

3   I know I can't always trust my gut feelings. **In spite of this / By the same token**, they play a big part in my decision-making.

4   Love and empathy are considered positive emotions. **Equally / Despite this**, gratitude and joy enhance a person's life.

5   Empathy motivates people to help others. **On the contrary / By the same token**, guilt strengthens commitment to others.

6   Anger makes it harder for people to change what they are already doing, **similarly / whereas** fear makes them give up too easily.

7   A fearful person is less likely to take risks. **Similarly / On the contrary**, happy people are not risk-takers.

8   I sometimes jump into situations without considering all my options. **In the same way / In spite of this**, I sometimes find it hard to slow down and make intellectual decisions.

Academic words

1 Match the words in bold with the correct definitions.

1	**abstract** (adj)	a	to get the most benefit from
2	**categories** (n)	b	alone; not involving anything or anyone else
3	**complex** (adj)	c	groups of people or things that have similar qualities
4	**depressed** (adj)		
5	**interpret** (v)	d	consisting of several different parts; not simple
6	**maximize** (v)	e	to explain or figure out the meaning of something
7	**reluctant** (adj)	f	existing as an idea, but not having a physical form
8	**solely** (adv)	g	unwilling; not happy about doing something
		h	sad; unhappy

2 Complete the sentences with words from Exercise 1. Change the form if necessary.

1 When it rains for too many days in a row, I get _____. I need some sunshine to feel cheerful again.

2 Hamid was _____ responsible for the success of that project. Nobody else helped him.

3 I'm not sure how to _____ the results of this experiment. I don't know what they mean.

4 Businesses typically look for ways to _____ profits.

5 I'm _____ to take another literature course from that professor. I didn't enjoy the last one.

6 Some psychologists have tried to organize our emotions into different _____.

7 Introducing new regulations in the workplace is a _____ process.

8 Concepts like "truth" and "love" are hard to define because they're _____ ideas.

3 Work with a partner. Discuss the questions.

1 What would you do if someone who worked for you exhibited signs of depression?

2 Some people are reluctant to talk about their emotions and abstract ideas, while others enjoy talking things over with other people and interpreting their feelings. Which type of person are you more like?

Critical thinking

False analogy

An analogy is an extended comparison that tries to help you understand a new situation by comparing it to a familiar situation. However, you must analyze analogies carefully to make sure they are really comparing two similar situations.

> It's crucial for managers to take the emotional intelligence of their employees into account as well as intellectual intelligence when making decisions about staffing and promotions. Ignoring emotional intelligence would be like serving dinner without dessert. Managers should get targeted training in recognizing and developing emotional intelligence.

1 **Work with a partner. Discuss the questions.**

   1 What is the analogy? That is, what two situations are being compared?

   2 Do you think the analogy is accurate? Why / why not?

2 **Evaluate the following analogies. Check (✓) any that you think are sound.**

Not taking emotional intelligence into consideration when promoting a worker is like …

   1 ☐ creating a basketball team with only short people.

   2 ☐ making a color wheel with only blue and red, but not yellow.

   3 ☐ making a cup of coffee, but not adding any milk or cream.

   4 ☐ reading popular books, but not classic literature.

   5 ☐ trying to learn how to play the violin without learning how to read music.

3 Write your own analogy for the situation in Exercise 2. Then share it with a partner or group. Do they think it is sound?

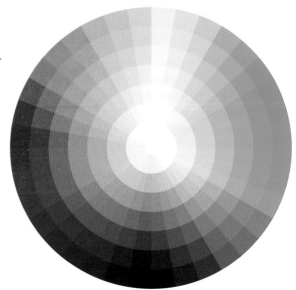

Writing model

You are going to learn about hedging statements to make them more accurate, and organizing a compare-and-contrast essay. You are then going to use these to write an essay about emotional and intellectual intelligence.

A Model

Read the essay prompt. Brainstorm ideas for the two categories.

"Which has a greater influence on a person's personality, nature or nurture?"

Nature	Nurture

B Analyze

Read the student model and answer the questions.

Is nature or nurture more important in forming someone's personality? It is tempting to say "both," but nevertheless I believe that of the two, nurture is more important. We can understand why by examining the areas of family influence and peer influence.

A person is born with certain physical characteristics—eye color, hair color, and height, for example. While I do believe it's true that children are born with personality traits, like patience, stubbornness, and curiosity, it is their parents and other authority figures who reinforce or discourage these traits. A parent can encourage, discourage, or ignore a child's behaviors, which will almost always influence how likely a child is to behave in the same way again.

Some people point to the different personalities of twins as proof that nature is more important. They offer examples of two children who were raised in the same house with the same parents, but still developed different personalities. However, in most cases, I believe this, too, is a result of nurture. After all, for the most part, even twins have different teachers, different coaches, different friends, and of course, different experiences. So these different outside influences will have different effects on children, even those who share almost all the same genes. This shows that for the most part outside factors have more influence on a person's personality than what they were born with.

1   What was the writer's answer to the question?

2   How many supporting points did the writer give? Where do you find this out?

3   Can you predict the order of the body paragraphs from the introduction? How?

Grammar

Adverbs for hedging

Especially when referring to people, it is difficult to make definite statements about what is true 100% of the time. To be more accurate, writers *hedge*, or modify the strength of their statements. Here are some hedging devices:

- adverbs such as *probably, maybe, perhaps, likely*
- adverbs such as *some, most, a few, about, approximately, somewhat, predominantly*
- adverbial phrases such as *in some cases, for some people, most of the time, for the most part*

1 **Reorder the words to make sentences.**

1 both walk and talk / at an earlier age / than boys / girls / most

Most _____

2 sunshine / many / somewhat depressed / the lack of / in the / people feel / winter because of

Many _____

3 that the power / people believe / any illness / almost / of thought / can cure / some

Some _____

4 the afternoon / for some / middle of / people, thinking / more difficult in the / can be

For _____

5 positive thinking / every student / teachers believe that / most / almost / get better results / can help

Most _____

6 can be / more logically / taught to / in most / think / cases, people

In _____

2 **Add a hedging adverb or adverbial to the following definite statements. Then compare with a partner.**

1 People think better during the day if they eat breakfast.

2 Thinking too much at night makes it difficult to sleep.

3 Bilingual people have thoughts in one language they don't have in the other.

4 Teens develop abstract thinking at age 12.

5 Right-brained people are good at playing music.

Writing skill

You have two possibilities when writing a compare-and-contrast essay.

Point-by-point: You write about the first aspect of A, and compare it to B. Then you write about the second aspect of A, and compare it to B. Then you write about the third aspect of A, and compare it to B.

Block: You write about all aspects of A. Then you write about all aspects of B.

With either organization, remember to draw a conclusion at the end.

1   Read the model essay on page 57 again. Does it use point-by-point organization or block organization?

2   Complete the outline for the model essay.

I   Introduction. Thesis statement: _____
   II   _____
        A _____
        B _____
   III   _____
        A _____
        B _____
   IV   Conclusion _____
   _____

Writing task

You are going to write an essay in response to the following:

"Which is more important in the workplace: emotional intelligence or intellectual intelligence?

Brainstorm

Use a double-columned chart to brainstorm ideas about emotional intelligence and intellectual intelligence in the workplace.

Plan

Choose which side you support. Decide whether you will use point-by-point organization or block organization. Write a brief outline for your essay.

Write

Use your brainstorm to help you write your essay. Remember to hedge your statements where appropriate, and to organize your ideas. Your text should be 250 words long.

Share

Exchange your essay with a partner. Use the checklist on page 189 to help you provide feedback to your partner.

Rewrite and edit

Consider your partner's comments and write your final draft. Think about:

- whether you answered the question clearly
- whether you used adverbs to hedge where appropriate
- whether you used clear organization.

Review

Wordlist

MACMILLAN DICTIONARY

Vocabulary preview

anxiety (n) **	encounter (v) **	point of view (n) **
concrete (adj) **	guilt (n) **	rational (adj) **
constantly (adv) **	hypothesize (v)	sort (v) ***
deadline (n) *	inappropriate (adj) **	strengthen (v) **
emotions (n) ***	logical (adj) **	

Vocabulary development

by the same token (phrase)	equally (adv) ***	on the contrary (phrase)
despite (prep) ***	in spite of (phrase)	similarly (adv) ***
	in the same way (phrase)	whereas (conj) ***

Academic words

abstract (adj) **	depressed (adj) **	reluctant (adj) **
categories (n)	interpret (v) ***	solely (adv) **
complex (adj) ***	maximize (v)	

Academic words review

Complete the sentences with the words in the box.

abstract	complex	interpret	maximize	notion

1   I disagree with the _____ that emotional response is based on experience.

2   This kind of difficult problem is too _____ for a child to solve.

3   A mature person is someone who can _____ their own emotions.

4   Most children are not able to think logically about _____ or hypothetical ideas.

5   Emotional thinking doesn't _____ a person's ability to work effectively.

Unit review

Reading 1	☐	I can understand ellipsis.
Reading 2	☐	I can understand the function of questions.
Study skill	☐	I can use association and mnemonics to improve my memory.
Vocabulary	☐	I can use language for comparing and contrasting.
Grammar	☐	I can use language for hedging.
Writing	☐	I can organize a compare-and-contrast essay.

Discussion point

Discuss with a partner.

1 Did any information in the chart surprise you?
   I was surprised that so much forestland is owned by …

2 Who should be responsible for making laws that protect forestland?
   I think the federal government should be responsible because …

3 Do you think owners of private lands should follow the same rules for taking care of forests as people who use public lands?
   I think private landowners should …

Who owns U.S. forests?

- federal government
- local government
- private businesses, organizations, and Native American tribes
- private families and individuals
- state government

3%

7%

21%

35%

34%

Information from the U.S. Department of Agriculture & the U.S. Forest Service.

VIDEO

SLASH AND BURN

Before you watch

Match the words in bold with the correct definitions.

1 **acute** (adj)   a related to breathing air in and out
2 **enforce** (v)   b the distance that you can see
3 **respiratory** (adj)   c very serious or severe
4 **smog** (n)   d to make sure that a rule or law is obeyed
5 **visibility** (n)   e polluted air; a mixture of smoke and fog

UNIT
AIMS

READING 1 Using word parts to understand meaning
READING 2 Recognizing sentence modifiers
STUDY SKILL Smart reading

VOCABULARY Vocabulary for talking about wildfires
GRAMMAR Gerunds as subjects
WRITING Organizing an argument essay

A firefighter in Phelan, California.

While you watch

Watch the video. Choose the correct answer.

1 The fires have been caused by a **natural phenomenon** / **man-made process**.

2 Many tour groups have **cancelled** / **delayed** their trips to Pekanbaru.

3 The negative health effects of smog **are** / **aren't** severe.

4 Current laws need to **be enforced** / **change**.

After you watch

Work with a partner. Discuss the questions.

1 What incentives could be given to companies to stop them using slash and burn?

    They could be offered …

2 What are the main environmental threats in your country?

    I think the main threats are … because …

3 What can you do to help protect the environment in your country?

    We should …

The top five causes of wildfires

A Vocabulary preview

Complete the sentences with a word from the box. Change the form if necessary.

beneficial   costly   enforce   maintenance   melt   rural   supervise   wilderness

1 It's important to _____ young children at all times so they don't get into trouble.

2 Wildfires are often a result of a failure to _____ local laws.

3 Wildfires are becoming more _____. In 2015 alone, the United States spent over $3 billion fighting wildfires.

4 Recent studies suggest wildfires may be causing ice in Greenland _____.

5 The state of Alaska, which has a very low human population, contains a little more than half of the United States' _____.

6 Proper use and _____ of equipment is key to wildfire prevention.

7 Wildfires in _____ areas can destroy entire communities.

8 Wildfires can actually be hugely _____ to the local environment.

B Before you read

Activating prior knowledge

The reading discusses five causes of wildfires. Predict how common they are by ranking the causes from 5 (least common) to 1 (most common).

___ backyard burning

___ cigarettes

___ sparks from equipment

___ unattended campfires

___ unsupervised activities

C Global reading

Reading for tone

Read *The top five causes of wildfires.* Answer the questions.

1 What is the main purpose of the reading?
   a to entertain   b to persuade   c to inform

2 Who is the audience for the reading?
   a Forest Service employees   b the general public   c lawmakers

3 What is the tone of the reading?
   a very informal   b somewhat informal   c formal

The top five causes of wildfires

1 How is it, that if you drop a cigarette in a wet forest it starts a fire by accident, but when you're camping and trying to set a fire on purpose, with dry wood and plenty of matches, you can't do it?

2 Personal fire-making skills aside, the causes of wildfires—defined as large, rapidly spreading fires especially in rural areas—are worth understanding. If we know what causes fires, we can work to prepare for them, and hopefully, prevent them.

3 Wildfires are both destructive and costly—and they're getting worse. Over the past few years, the number of wildfires has increased around the world, especially in countries with large forests such as Russia and Canada. One country in particular that is facing wildfire problems is the United States. In fact, every state in the western United States has seen an increase in the number of wildfires. They occur up to five times more often than 10 or 20 years ago. The fires burn for longer, too, and last nearly five times as long, and cover six times as much land. In 2015, more than ten million acres of land burned—an area about the size of the entire country of Switzerland. The amount of money spent to put out these fires is climbing to two billion dollars a year.

4 What's causing this? Fires have to be started by a trigger—that is, something that begins the fire. This can be by humans, either on purpose or by accident, or something natural, such as by lightning. But events like these have always happened. Why are they leading to more fires now?

5 The main answer is global warming, a gradual heating of the planet. This affects forests in several ways. First of all, a warmer climate means a drier climate because more water evaporates. Snow in mountain areas melts earlier, so the ground is drier for a longer period of time. Together, these factors increase the risk of a chance spark growing into a wildfire. Furthermore, when fires start, because the ground is drier, they burn hotter, spread faster, and last longer. And they're more difficult to contain or extinguish. Wildfires in large forests can burn for several months.

6 Climate change affects fires in other ways too. When the balance of nature in a forest changes, trees become weak or sick. Insects and other animals damage the weakened trees, which can die, and dead trees become a fuel source for fires. Lightning strikes the earth more than 100,000 times a day, and 10–20% of these events are capable of starting a fire. It's clear that steps need to be taken to reduce this risk.

7 However, about 90% of all wildfires are started by humans. In theory, it should be easier to reduce this number than the number of lightning strikes. Let's take a closer look at some of the causes.

8 The fifth most common cause of wildfires started by humans is backyard burning—fires that people set to burn garden waste or trash. These fires may be set following local laws, but then grow too large, are spread by wind, or are not put out correctly. Local laws need to be clarified and properly enforced to reduce risky behavior.

9 The fourth most common cause is sparks from equipment such as cars, trucks, or farm machinery. Proper maintenance is essential to stop machines from starting a fire.

10 Cigarettes are the third leading cause of wildfires. Education campaigns that teach fire safety are a good way to address this problem.

11 Second is unsupervised activities, such as children playing with matches or people setting off fireworks. Education is important but not sufficient in the case of young children. They need to be supervised at all times by parents or other adults and kept away from fuel and things that start fires.

12 And first? The main cause of human-caused wildfires is campfires that are either not in a safe area, get out of control, or aren't put out properly. Campers and outdoor enthusiasts need to learn where and when it is safe to build a campfire and how to make sure the fire is completely out before they leave the area.

13 It is true that some fires in wilderness areas can have beneficial effects too, such as helping new trees and plants to grow. However, because recent wildfires burn hotter and longer, these effects don't always occur. Instead, we lose land, animal and plant life, and a lot of money. As the earth grows warmer, we need to work harder to protect forests from wildfires.

GLOSSARY

acre (n) a unit for measuring the surface area of land, equal to 4,047 square meters

evaporate (v) if liquid evaporates it changes into gas or steam

sparks (n) a very small piece of burning material

Using word parts to understand meaning

D Close reading

Word parts can be divided into three useful categories, all of which are found in the word *prevention*:

- roots, which show meaning   *ven* = come
- prefixes, which modify meaning   *pre-* = before; in advance
- suffixes, which show the part of speech   *-tion* = noun

Knowing that *pre-* means "in advance" and *ven* means "come" makes it easier to remember that *prevent* means "stopping something in advance before it comes (happens)."

1   Read *The top five causes of wildfires* again. Match words in the text to the roots below. Then write the meaning of the word. Use a dictionary if necessary.

   1   *grad-*, a step (example: *graduate*)

      paragraph 5: word: _____ meaning: _____

   2   *cap-*, to take or hold (example: *capacity*)

      paragraph 6: word: _____ meaning: _____

   3   *duc-*, to lead or bring (example: *induce*)

      paragraph 6: word: _____ meaning: _____

   4   *clar-*, to make clear (example: *declare*)

      paragraph 8: word: _____ meaning: _____

   5   *vis-*, see or watch (example: *visual*)

      paragraph 11: word: _____ meaning: _____

2   Read the text again and find different forms of the words. Use suffixes from the box to help you.

Adjective	Adverb
-al	-ly
-ive	-ward
-y	
Noun	**Verb**
-ity	-ate
-ment	-ify
-tion	-ize
-ure	

1   The adverb form of *rapid*:

2   The adjective form of *destruction*:

3   The noun form of *natural*:

4   The adjective form of *location*:

5   The noun form of *equip*:

6   The adjective form of *risk*:

7   The adverb form of *proper*:

E Critical thinking

Work in a group. Discuss the questions.

1   According to the article, 90% of forest fires are caused by humans. Do you think they all could have been prevented? Why / why not?

2   Whose responsibility is it to prevent forest fires: individuals, organizations, or the government?

Study skills   Smart reading

Chart the main ideas

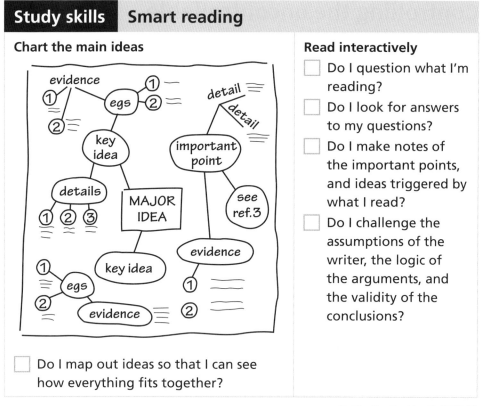

Do I map out ideas so that I can see how everything fits together?

Read interactively

☐ Do I question what I'm reading?

☐ Do I look for answers to my questions?

☐ Do I make notes of the important points, and ideas triggered by what I read?

☐ Do I challenge the assumptions of the writer, the logic of the arguments, and the validity of the conclusions?

© Stella Cottrell (2013)

1 Read the *Smart reading* box. Check (✓) the questions you already ask when reading an academic text. Then explain to a partner how you address each point.

2 Work with a partner. Discuss the questions.

   1 Why is it important to read actively? What are some disadvantages to not reading actively?

   2 Do you think it's important to do all of the interactive reading techniques, or only some of them?

3 Which of the questions would an interactive reader have asked about *The top five causes of wildfires*? Check (✓) your answers.

   1 ☐ What are the top five causes of forest fires?
   2 ☐ Why is it important to know the causes of forest fires?
   3 ☐ How many acres of land burned in 2015?
   4 ☐ Why is the number of forest fires increasing?
   5 ☐ How many forest fires are caused by humans?
   6 ☐ Why don't some parents supervise their children?
   7 ☐ How many laws are there to stop people from causing fires?

4 Work with a partner and discuss your answers to Exercise 3. Explain your reasoning.

Controlling the uncontrollable

A Vocabulary preview

1 Match the words in bold with the correct definitions.

1	**conduct** (v)	a	to use something for a particular purpose
2	**employ** (v)	b	to put out a fire
3	**extinguish** (v)	c	used for describing an earlier period of time
4	**historically** (adv)	d	used to describe the later part of a period of time
5	**latter** (adj)	e	to do something in an organized way
6	**renew** (v)	f	to replace something that is damaged or old
7	**threaten** (v)	g	to be likely to harm or damage something
8	**vegetation** (n)	h	plants and trees

2 Complete the sentences with words from Exercise 1. Change the form if necessary.

1 Forest fires _____ local communities and destroy large areas of farmland.

2 _____, forest fires were largely caused by natural events.

3 Firefighters _____ a number of different methods for dealing with forest fires.

4 Forest fires help _____ and maintain healthy ecosystems.

5 It took firefighters several weeks _____ the fire.

6 How quickly _____ recovers after a wildfire depends on the weather conditions at that time of year.

7 Human-caused forest fires increased rapidly in the _____ half of the 20th century.

8 Schools in the area _____ forest fire exercises once a week.

B Before you read

Activating prior knowledge

Work with a partner. Discuss why you think Forest Service workers might deliberately set forest fires.

C Global reading

Skimming

Skim *Controlling the uncontrollable* and answer the questions.

1 The main topic is *controlled burns*. What paragraph defines this term?

2 What is the function of the paragraphs that come before the definition?

3 What is the function of the paragraphs that come after the definition?

Controlling the uncontrollable

1 **Northern New Mexico, in the southwestern United States, is a near-perfect setting for a forest fire. It's warm, it's dry, and the trees that grow there burn hot and fast. Historically, fires occurred naturally every few years, usually as a result of lightning strikes. These fires would clear out old, dead wood and renew the land.**

2 However, after settling in the area and starting to build homes and graze livestock, people worked hard to prevent such fires. Understandably, homeowners and farmers didn't want to risk their property or their lives. Yet without smaller, more frequent fires to remove the dead wood and grass, once a wildfire did start, it burned much hotter and longer. In the latter half of the 20th century, such fires occurred about every 20 years. Two of these, the 1977 La Mesa Fire and the 1996 Dome Fire, were particularly strong. They both threatened the nearby town of Los Alamos, home to some 15,000 residents and a scientific laboratory, the Los Alamos National Laboratory, which conducts research for the military.

3 In the years following the 1996 Dome Fire, when the flames could be seen from the streets of Los Alamos, weather patterns changed. First came a few unusually wet years, which meant more plants, bushes, and trees grew. Then came a few years of drought, which killed much of the vegetation and dried it out. The result was like stacking dry firewood under the trees.

4 Reviewing the landscape and taking into account the cycles of large, hot wildfires that swept through the canyons, employees of the National Park Service at Bandelier National Monument, a park known for its wildlife and archaeological sites, made a decision—and nearly destroyed Los Alamos.

5 If you know you have a large area of land where a fire is likely to occur, and that the fire can easily spread, what can you do about it? Without the benefit of small, natural fires to clear out the dead plants, the Park Service mistakenly decided to employ a technique called a "controlled burn." This technique involves deliberately setting a fire that will burn only in an area chosen and monitored by firefighters. Around this area, all the vegetation will be removed, creating what's known as a "fire break" that the fire can't cross.

6 Once it has done its job—clearing away dead trees and fallen plants—the fire will be extinguished, leaving an area that is now at far less risk to a wildfire. Setting a fire on purpose allows firefighters to control how long it burns and how far it spreads, which makes it a valuable tool for forest management. At least, that's the theory.

7 Late in the evening of May 4, 2000, Park Service employees set the fire. By late morning the next day, however, the fire had jumped over the firebreaks on one side due to high winds. On May 10, the fire spread into Los Alamos Canyon and headed towards the town and the laboratory and its facilities.

8 Fortunately, the town's 18,000 residents were all evacuated, and no lives were lost. However, 280 homes were destroyed or damaged, leaving 400 residents homeless. The fire reached the laboratory, and burned 40 buildings. Residents were allowed to return on May 18, although the fire was not completely extinguished until July 20. But the consequences were bad enough. The largest and most destructive fire in the history of New Mexico, the Cerro Grande fire, burned 47,000 acres of land and cost an estimated $906 million.

9 The officials in charge of the Cerro Grande "controlled burn" acknowledged they'd made some mistakes and lost their jobs, and new regulations for "controlled burns" were passed. Nearly a decade after the fire, plants and animals have returned to the area, though the effects of the fire are still there today.

10 Today, many "controlled burns" go as planned, and admittedly, may save the forests from natural disasters. But clearly, questions remain. Are these burns an essential part of federal forest management? Or are they simply too risky? Does the danger of natural fires in the future justify the danger of manmade fires in the present? Opponents point to incidents like Cerro Grande as evidence that fire and wind are unpredictable, and that errors can be costly. They suggest other methods to clear dead trees, such as removing them by machine. Supporters say "controlled burns" are used effectively most of the time, and that the consequences of not using such solutions are potentially far worse. Slower methods, such as using machinery, leave forests vulnerable to natural fires for longer amounts of time and also cost a lot more; nothing is as cheap and fast as a "controlled burn". Obviously, both sides share the same goal—to keep forests healthy and whole, and to protect the surrounding communities.

GLOSSARY

unpredictable (adj)
changing often, in a way that is impossible to prepare for

D Close reading

> It's often possible to identify an author's point of view using adverbs in the text:
>
> **Fortunately**, *nobody was killed in the fire.* (= the author thinks it's lucky that nobody was killed)
>
> *Local residents were **understandably** relieved.* (= the author empathizes with the local residents)

Read *Controlling the uncontrollable* again. Match the points of view to sentences in the text.

1 The writer can relate to residents wanting to protect themselves and their property.
2 The writer thinks the Park Service's use of the "controlled burn" was a bad idea.
3 The writer feels it was lucky none of the local residents were killed.
4 The writer accepts that controlled fires may benefit forests.
5 The writer thinks it's clear supporters and opponents of "controlled burns" want the same thing.

E Critical thinking

Work in a group. Discuss the questions.

1 The Cerro Grande fire was set deliberately, yet the people who set it were trained professionals who were trying to do something beneficial. Should they have been punished? Why / why not? If so, what sort of punishment do you think is appropriate?
2 What factors should be taken into account when considering forest management: money, resources, benefits gained, possible risks, other factors?
3 Who should be responsible for taking care of large areas of wilderness? Who should be responsible for paying for that care?

Vocabulary development

Collocations with *problem*

1 Choose the correct definition for each collocation.

1 The root of the **problem**
   a the problem's fundamental cause
   b the smallest aspect of a problem

2 To cope with a **problem**
   a to deal with a problem
   b to give up on dealing with a problem

3 To remedy a **problem**
   a to cause a problem
   b to solve a problem

4 To be faced with **problems**
   a to encounter problems
   b to be overcome by problems

5 A pressing **problem**
   a a problem that must be solved soon
   b a problem that causes great stress

6 A minor **problem**
   a a problem that makes people sad
   b a problem that is not very serious

7 A grave **problem**
   a a rare or unusual problem
   b a very serious problem

8 A perennial **problem**
   a a problem that is not so serious
   b a problem that happens again and again

2 Work in a group. Discuss the questions using information from the texts to help you.

1 What are some perennial problems that forests are faced with? Why do you think they are perennial? Which is the gravest?

2 Think about the leading causes of fires. Which do you think are the most pressing? How would you remedy those problems?

3 What do you think is the root of the problem of prescribed burns that get out of control? How do you think the Forest Service can cope with that problem?

Academic words

1 Match the words in bold with the correct definitions.

1 **acknowledge** (v)   a a period of ten years
2 **capable** (adj)   b an official rule that controls how something is done
3 **decade** (n)   c able to do something
4 **error** (n)   d to admit or accept that something is true
5 **federal** (adj)   e a mistake
6 **regulation** (n)   f relating to a national government

2 Complete the sentences with words from Exercise 1. Change the form if necessary.

1 The National Park Service defines a fuel as any material _____ of burning.
2 Local, state, and _____ governments should work together to protect public land.
3 An estimated 90% of forest fires are caused by human _____.
4 Tighter camping _____ might help reduce numbers of forest fires in the area.
5 This land has been privately owned for several _____.
6 The Forest Service _____ that prescribed burns can be risky.

3 Work with a partner. Discuss the questions.

1 What regulations do you think the government should introduce to reduce the possibility of forest fires caused by human error?

   Regulations
   1 First, the government should ... _____
   _____
   2 Secondly, it is vital for the government to ... _____
   _____
   3 Finally, the government should be required to ... _____
   _____

2 Do you think the federal government should acknowledge any mistakes at the time they are made, or is it acceptable to wait a decade or more?

Critical thinking

Questioning assumptions

Good arguments should be supported with evidence. However, if it's reasonable to assume that most readers will agree with your position, it may not be necessary to support your argument:

Obviously, prescribed forest fires cannot be allowed to burn unattended.

As most people would agree that prescribed forest fires should not be left unattended, the writer doesn't need to provide evidence to support this position.

However, sometimes writers make assumptions that not everyone would agree with:

Clearly, global warming has no effect on forest fires.

As many people would disagree with this point of view, the writer needs to provide supporting evidence to strengthen their argument.

Questioning assumptions will help you to evaluate the strength of a writer's argument.

1   **Read the text and underline the assumptions.**

We all agree that the problem of forest fires is growing. Obviously, something needs to be done about it. For years, the Forest Service in our state has worked to prevent forest fires from happening or to suppress or control fires that do start. Some people argue for a more aggressive program of prescribed burns. But after the disastrous fire of 2016, surely we can see that none of these methods can work. Rather than try to keep fires away from people's homes, it's clear that what we should do instead is keep homes away from forests. If we passed a law forbidding new home construction within 100 miles of a major forest, we could prevent houses from burning down should a fire occur.

2   **Work with a partner. Discuss the questions.**

1   Which of the assumptions are reasonable? Which are unreasonable? Why?

2   What kind of evidence could be used to support the unreasonable assumptions?

3   **Work in a group. Discuss the questions.**

1   Why is it dangerous to assume your readers agree with your position?

2   Apart from writers, what other kinds of people make statements they assume you'll agree with?

3   Is it ever useful to make assumptions? Why / why not?

Writing model

You are going to learn about using gerunds as the subject of a sentence, and supporting your arguments. You are then going to use these to write an essay about fire prevention.

A Analyze

Read the essay prompt. Brainstorm ideas for the problem and the solution.

"The number of wildfires is increasing around the world. What are the reasons for this? What solutions can you suggest to cope with this problem?"

Problems	Solutions

B Model

Read the student model and answer the questions.

Forest fires around the world are increasing not only in frequency but also in severity. To save our forests and the communities near them, we need to identify the major causes of forest fires and implement some solutions.

The root of the problem is either natural causes, such as lightning strikes, or human causes, such as campfires or fireworks. Preventing lightning is not possible, of course, but we can work harder to prevent human-caused fires, such as by increasing educational programs, making it a crime to engage in dangerous behavior in or near a forest, and hiring more staff at national parks to keep an eye on visitors.

However, I believe what we need most of all is to maintain healthy forests that are less at risk to fires. Using prescribed burns is one method, but these burns can be dangerous too. Even if the number of times Forest Service staff members lose control of a prescribed burn is low, each time it happens, the consequences are severe.

Developing healthier forests is a better remedy. Over the years, forests have become overcrowded, and sometimes people have planted the wrong kinds of trees and other plants. If Forest Service personnel cleared out old, dead wood, cut down some trees so the forest was not too crowded, and removed non-native species of plants, this would result in healthier forests. Then, even if a fire started, it would be a minor problem, and not a grave one, and firefighters would be able to cope with it.

Even if the solution takes more time and money than prescribed burns, the benefits in the long term are worth it.

1 What did the writer identify as the problem(s) and solution(s)?
2 Why doesn't the writer recommend prescribed burns?
3 What type of support is not used in the essay?
4 What does the conclusion do?

Grammar

Gerunds and reduced clauses

When you see a word ending in -ing at the beginning of a sentence, it is usually:

- a gerund, a type of noun
  Setting fires in windy weather is dangerous.

or

- part of a reduced clause
  Burning all night, the fire destroyed 50 acres of land.

Note that there is no comma after the gerund, whereas there is one after the reduced clause. Use punctuation clues to help you understand the part of speech.

When using a gerund as a subject, remember that it is singular, and therefore takes a singular verb.

1 Check (✓) the sentences that have gerunds as subjects.

1 ☐ Supervising children around campfires is very important.

2 ☐ Having carefully extinguished the fire, the campers went to bed.

3 ☐ Knowing when the conditions are safe for a prescribed burn is not easy.

4 ☐ Understanding how wildfires are necessary for forest health can be taught in schools.

5 ☐ Studying the wind conditions, the Forest Service concluded that the prescribed burn should be delayed.

6 ☐ Allowing fires to start naturally is not practical in sectors where a lot of people now live.

2 Rewrite the sentences in your notebook to begin with a gerund. The first one has been done as an example.

1 It is important to teach fire safety to everyone.
   Teaching fire safety to everyone is important.

2 It is necessary to ban smoking in forests.

3 It will help people understand fire to read this article.

4 It was unfortunate to lose so many acres of land to wildfires.

5 It's important to study how erosion happens in the wilderness.

6 It will be expensive to train new park service employees.

Writing skill

To convince readers that your arguments are sound, you must support those arguments. Three common ways to do this are with:

- reasons
- examples
- quotes or expert testimony

Write one or two pieces of support into your outline before you begin your first draft. This will ensure that your arguments are well supported.

1 **Read the model essay again. Then answer the questions.**

1 In paragraph 2, what examples does the writer give of natural causes of fires and of human causes?

2 In paragraph 3, how does the writer support the argument against prescribed burns?

3 In paragraph 4, what types of support are used?

2 **Match the arguments (1–4) with the supporting information (a–d).**

1 Campfires should be prohibited in all forests. ___

2 Climate change is having a direct effect on the number of forest fires in the United States. ___

3 Using controlled burns to remove unwanted plants and trees helps stop fires from spreading. ___

4 Not allowing forest fires to burn out naturally has a negative impact on the ecosystem. ___

a A recent study showed a positive correlation between increased global temperatures and instances of forest fire.

b Many plants have adapted to actually release their seeds when burned. Without forest fires, these plants will simply die out.

c As many as 90% of wildfires in the United States are caused by human activity, such as not extinguishing campfires properly.

d Conrad McCarthy of the Mayweather Institute recently stated, *"Clearing vegetation removes a fire's primary fuel source, and can massively slow its progress."*

3 **Work with a partner. Write sentences to support the following arguments:**

1 Current techniques for controlling and extinguishing fires work.

2 Forest fires have a positive effect on the environment.

3 Campsites should provide better information on the safe use of fire.

Writing task

You are going to write a problem / solution essay in response to the following: *"Preventing campfires from causing wildfires is a major challenge. What are some reasons for this? What can be done to solve this problem?"*

Brainstorm

Make a two-column chart such as the one on page 68 and list problems with campfires and possible solutions.

Plan

From your brainstorm, choose your arguments. Write 1 to 2 pieces of support for each one. You can use information from *Reading 1*, *Writing skill*, and your own knowledge.

Write

Use your brainstorm to help you write your essay. Remember to use gerunds and reduced clauses where appropriate, and to support your argument. Your text should be 250 words long.

Share

Exchange your essay with a partner. Use the checklist on page 189 to help you provide feedback to your partner.

Rewrite and edit

Consider your partner's comments and write your final draft. Think about:

- whether you answered the question clearly
- whether you discussed both problems and solutions
- whether you used gerunds and reduced clauses appropriately
- whether you supported your arguments appropriately.

Review

Wordlist

MACMILLAN
DICTIONARY

Vocabulary preview

beneficial (adj) **	historically (adv) *	supervise (v) **
conduct (v) ***	latter (adj) ***	threaten (v) ***
costly (adj) *	maintenance (n) **	vegetation (n)
employ (v) ***	melt (v) **	wilderness (n)
enforce (v) **	renew (v) **	
extinguish (v)	rural (adj) ***	

Vocabulary development

cope (v) ***	minor (adj) *	problem (n) ***
face (v) ***	perennial (adj)	remedy (v) *
grave (adj) *	pressing (adj)	root (n) ***

Academic words

acknowledge (v) **	decade (n) ***	federal (adj) **
capable (adj) ***	error (n) ***	regulation (n) ***

Academic words review

Complete the sentences with the words in the box.

capable	depressed	error	federal	solely

1 The Park Service shouldn't rely _____ on the "controlled burn" technique.

2 It's hard not to feel _____ about the effects of global warming.

3 Many things are _____ of starting a wildfire other than lightning.

4 When it comes to fire prevention, even the smallest _____ can have grave consequences.

5 The _____ government is responsible for all the forests in this area.

Unit review

Reading 1 ☐ I can use word parts to understand meaning.

Reading 2 ☐ I can recognize sentence modifiers.

Study skill ☐ I can use Smart Reading techniques.

Vocabulary ☐ I can use vocabulary for talking about wildfires.

Writing ☐ I can organize an argument essay.

Grammar ☐ I can use gerunds as subjects.

5 MOVEMENT

International Shipping

About **90%** of world trade is carried by international shipping trade

There are over **50,000** merchant ships trading internationally

Some large hi-tech vessels can cost over **$200 million**

Shipping is more environmentally friendly than road vehicles and air transport:
CO² emissions:
A very large shipping vessel = **3.0 grams** of CO_2 per tonne-km
Air freight = **435 grams** of CO_2 per tonne-km

Discussion point

Discuss with a partner.

1　What in the infographic surprised you?

I was surprised by …

2　What different goods do you think are most commonly shipped around the world?

I think …

3　Is it important to try and reduce the number of goods transported around the world? Why / why not?

In my opinion …

I don't think …

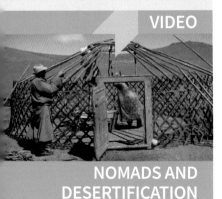

VIDEO

NOMADS AND DESERTIFICATION

Before you watch

Match the words in bold with the correct definitions.

1	**desertification** (n)	a	a group of people who live together
2	**sparse** (adj)	b	the process of turning fertile land to desert
3	**to graze** (v)	c	thin and hard to find
4	**to reclaim** (v)	d	to eat grass in a field
5	**tribe** (n)	e	to take back

UNIT
AIMS

READING 1 Annotating a text
READING 2 Recognizing text structure
STUDY SKILL Setting priorities

VOCABULARY Vocabulary for describing change
GRAMMAR Future passive
WRITING Comparing maps

Container ship in open water.

While you watch

Watch the video and choose the correct option to complete the sentences.

1 The video is about **the impact of desertification / reclaiming desert land**.

2 The people in the video moved to the cities because **they wanted to change their nomadic lifestyle / they couldn't live in their traditional way**.

3 The causes of desertification are **drought and overgrazing / unemployment and industrial development**.

4 This is **an international problem / just a national problem for Mongolia**.

After you watch

Work with a partner. Discuss the questions.

1 What do you know about nomadic people living in your country?

2 How do you think the lives of Dariimaa and Tsogldraleh are different now that they live near a city?

3 Should governments do more to support nomadic lifestyles? What can they do?

   Yes, I think they should … / No, I think …

The Panama Canal: A brief history

A Vocabulary preview

Complete the sentences with the words in the box.

cargo   circumnavigate   feat   fumigate   swamp   toll   treaty   zone

1 A _____ is a large, wet area of land filled with plants and wildlife.
2 The two countries signed a _____ to establish a border.
3 You must wear protective clothing in a construction _____.
4 Building a bridge or a dam is a significant _____ of engineering.
5 Some trains carry passengers, but many transport _____ instead.
6 To pay for the construction of the highway, each car had to pay a _____ in order to use it.
7 Ferdinand Magellan is considered to be the first person to _____ the Earth by sailing all around it.
8 We had to _____ our office to get rid of some insects.

B Before you read

Predicting

Without checking the text, predict answers to the following questions.

1 Why was the Panama Canal built?
2 What country began work on the Panama Canal? What country finished it?
3 What were the leading causes of death for workers on the Panama Canal?

C Global reading

Annotating a text

Annotating a text means marking and taking notes as you read. Methods include:
*   highlighting, circling, and underlining key information, such as important names, terms, and dates
*   writing notes in the margin to summarize main points and important information
*   writing questions in the margin to remind yourself to check information or look up further resources later

1 Read *The Panama Canal: A brief history*. Highlight important information, including answers to the questions in *B Before you read*.

2 Read the text again. Summarize the main idea of each paragraph in the margin.

The Panama Canal: A brief history

1 Once explorers had circumnavigated the world in the 1500s proving that the Earth was round and that other countries could be reached by ship, traders and travelers still had this problem: routes weren't always very convenient. If one wanted to sail from England to India, for example, that meant going 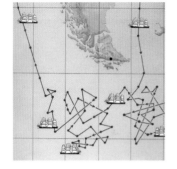 down around the Horn of Africa, a long and dangerous journey. Sailing from Spain to California, or even New York to California, meant sailing around Cape Horn at the southernmost tip of South America.

2 The construction of the Suez Canal in 1869 meant that ships could more easily pass between Europe and Asia. Attention then turned to Central America, the narrowest land barrier between the Atlantic and the Pacific Oceans.

3 Countries had actually been thinking about a canal in that region since the 1500s, and the Spanish explored the land with such a project in mind. However, they thought that it wouldn't be possible due to the mountains and jungles.

4 The first country to attempt a canal was France, using a team managed by Ferdinand de Lesseps, who had successfully built the Suez Canal. Work began in Panama in 1880, but the construction was not straightforward. The workers experienced great difficulties not only with the land but with the constant rains and malaria and yellow fever from the region's many mosquitos. Work was abandoned in 1888.

5 The United States was the next country to be interested. They purchased the Canal Zone from France in 1902. Unable to get permission to build in Colombia, they instead made a deal with the newly independent government of Panama in 1903.

6 Initially, the Americans experienced the same problems the French did. Success didn't come until they brought in new equipment, changed the design of the canal to a system of locks, and worked on the disease problem. The project's chief sanitary officer, Dr. William Gorgas, worked hard to reduce the number of mosquitos in the area. The connection between mosquitos and malaria had only been discovered in the late 1800s, and not everyone believed that Gorgas' work would make any difference. However, the last reported case of yellow fever in the area was in 1905, and malaria cases fell dramatically, thanks to Gorgas' efforts to get rid of swamps and small standing pools of water, fumigate areas where people lived, and encourage the use of mosquito netting.

7 Diseases were not the only challenge. In early 1907, the chief engineer of the project, John Frank Stevens, suddenly resigned. The reasons for this were never discovered. It is possible, though, that because he was a railroad engineer, he felt he didn't have the expertise necessary to build locks and dams. Nevertheless, before he left, he built essential support for the project, including warehouses and piers, as well as facilities for the workers and their families such as houses, hospitals, and schools.

8 George W. Goethals was chosen as the next chief engineer. One of his first projects was to clear a passage through a nine-mile (14-kilometer) stretch of mountains. It took around 6,000 men working around the clock to finish the Culebra Cut, as it became known. Men blasted through rock and earth, risking landslides, and removed the debris with trains—all told, more than 100 million cubic yards (76 million cubic meters) of material. They had to lay down more train track as they advanced. At the busiest times, a train either arrived or left almost every minute. It was considered one of the greatest engineering feats of the time.

9 In 1909, the construction of the locks was begun. Locks at each end of the canal raise ships to Gatun Lake, an artificial lake, and then lower the ships back down on the other side. The Panama Canal had its official opening on August 15, 1914. More recently, from 2007 to 2016, the canal was expanded to include a wider lock for larger, more modern ships.

10 In 1977, the United States signed a treaty to eventually return control of the land to Panama. For a certain period, the United States and Panama shared control of the canal, and then in 1999, Panama assumed full control. Tolls from the passing ships contribute about a billion dollars to the Panamanian economy each year.

11 In 1914, the year it opened, about 1,000 ships passed through the Panama Canal. The number steadily increased year by year. By 2014, about 14,000 ships a year were traversing the canal, and today, this figure is about 40 ships a day.

12 The cost of the Panama Canal was huge, both in money (the United States spent 8.6 billion dollars on the project) and human lives—in the first part of the project, 22,000 workers died, mostly from malaria or yellow fever. The American team lost 5,600 workers to accidents and disease.

13 The result? 48 miles (77 kilometers) that takes eight to ten hours to navigate, as opposed to 8,000 miles around Cape Horn. These days, it's estimated that 90% of all products are moved around the world by cargo ships. If you look around you, it's likely that something you see passed through the Panama Canal at some stage. So, whether you live near the canal or far away, it's probably influenced your life.

GLOSSARY

malaria (n) a serious illness caused by being bitten by a mosquito, usually in a hot country

D Close reading

1 Read this information from *The Panama Canal: A brief history*.
   Which paragraph contains each idea?

   a The most dangerous aspect of work in the canal zone was disease. ___

   b The Suez Canal links Europe and Asia. ___

   c The Panama Canal works by a series of locks. ___

   d The name of the southernmost tip of South America is Cape Horn. ___

   e Reducing or eliminating mosquitos was key to completing work on the
     canal. ___

   f The United States completed construction of the Panama Canal. ___

   g France began construction on the Panama Canal. ___

   h A majority of the world's goods is transported by ship. ___

2 Match the information below with the correct number in the box. One
   number is not used.

   | 77 | 1999 | 1880 | 1907 | 90 | 1977 | 6,000 | 1869 | 1914 | 8.6 | 1,000 |

   1 The year the Suez Canal was built _____

   2 The year work began on the Panama Canal _____

   3 The year John Frank Stevens resigned _____

   4 The number of workers who built the Culebra Cut _____

   5 The year the Panama Canal opened _____

   6 The cost in billions of dollars to the U.S. of the project _____

   7 The number of ships that passed through the first year _____

   8 The year Panama gained complete control of the canal _____

   9 The length of the canal, in kilometers _____

   10 The percent of products worldwide carried by cargo ships _____

E Critical thinking

Work in a group. Discuss the questions.

1 What are some reasons so many of the world's goods are transported by
   cargo ship?

2 What positive changes does faster, easier shipping bring to the world?
   Are there any negative changes?

3 How would your life change if shipping were slower and more expensive?

Study skills | Set your priorities

- [ ] 1 Write a "To do" list of everything you have to do.
- [ ] 2 Highlight or underline the essential tasks.
- [ ] 3 Identify the most urgent items on the list (those with the tightest deadline).
- [ ] 4 Identify the most important items on the list (those with the most serious consequences if not completed).
- [ ] 5 Number the items in the best order.
- [ ] 6 Work out how long you can spend on each one.
- [ ] 7 Decide what might have to be missed out.
- [ ] 8 Enter into your timetable or planner the times put aside for each stage of all essential tasks.

© Stella Cottrell (2013)

1 Read a university student's "To do" list. Number the tasks in order of priority. Are there any tasks that could be skipped? If so, which ones, and why? Discuss your choices with a partner.

_____ go to business class lecture

_____ take economics test

_____ study for midterm exams with Katie and Ji Eun

_____ exercise—walk? go to the gym?

_____ do laundry

_____ register for next semester—noon deadline!!

_____ call parents

_____ think about summer job—check job postings

2 Write a "To do" list for yourself for tomorrow or next week. Prioritize your list. Then share it with a partner. Explain how you made your choices.

Dangers and opportunities in the Arctic Circle

A Vocabulary preview

Complete the sentences with the words in the box. Change the form if necessary.

arise   coastal   dispute   halt   indigenous   marine   reef   sparse

1 Whales, sharks, and seals are examples of _____ animals.
2 When the project ran out of funds, construction was _____.
3 If the need _____, we can raise more funds to protect the land.
4 Areas with only a _____ amount of trees don't have as many birds.
5 Rabbits are not _____ to Australia. They were introduced by early settlers.
6 Many colorful fish live near the _____.
7 My neighbor and I have a _____ about the location of the fence between our yards.
8 Residents in _____ areas are sometimes threatened by storms at sea or large waves.

B Before you read

Preparing to read

Work with a partner. Brainstorm three problems connected with movement across extreme environments.

C Global reading

Recognizing text structure

As you read a text, think about the purpose of each paragraph. Annotate this in the margin. Then, when you are looking for specific information or reviewing for an exam, it will be easier to find the information you need by referring to your notes.

Read *Dangers and opportunities in the Arctic Circle*. Annotate the paragraphs (1–12) with the labels (a–l).

a background to the issue
b conclusion
c examples of benefits to less ice on the land
d changes to shipping routes (x2)
e how climate change affects the land
f how climate change affects the water

g the Arctic Council
h future challenges
i introduction
j land problems resulting from climate change
k water problems resulting from climate change
l which countries own the area

DANGERS AND OPPORTUNITIES
IN THE ARCTIC CIRCLE

1 While many people around the world debate the causes of climate change and whether it can be halted or reversed, others are already planning to deal with the consequences.

2 One area in which this is happening is the Arctic Circle, which is warming at a faster rate than the rest of the planet. In fact, climate scientists predict that this region could be completely free of ice in the summer months. The changes are bound to speed up too. The white ice and snow of the Arctic reflect sunlight back into space. In contrast, darker rock and bare earth absorb more of the sun's rays and warm the land.

3 As more land surface is not protected, the area is likely to suffer more forest fires and storm damage. Plant and animal species are certain to change, as some die off and others appear. Human populations will need to adjust as well, as coastal land disappears under rising waters. 81% of Greenland, for example, is covered by ice, which is melting at increasing rates. If all of that ice melted, the world's oceans would rise by seven meters. It is unlikely that all of Greenland's ice will melt, but it is certain that some of it will, which will flood some coastal towns. A rise in seawater levels could affect as many as 600 million people worldwide, and two-thirds of the world's largest cities.

4 At the same time, more land exposed in the Arctic means increased opportunities for the development of resources. Oil, natural gas, and minerals will be more easily accessible. In fact, by some estimates, the Arctic region contains as much as 25% of the world's undiscovered petroleum resources.

5 It's not just the land that is changing. The Arctic sea ice is also becoming thinner, which means it melts more easily. This creates a similar cycle to the one on the land: Less white ice and more dark water causes more sunlight to be absorbed, which speeds up the melting of more ice.

6 As sea temperatures rise, cold-water species of fish and sea animals are dying out. Diseases are spreading more rapidly, damaging coral reefs and marine life, especially shellfish.

7 When sea levels change, ships will be obliged to change their routes. New passageways could open up and make it easier for cargo ships to cross the Arctic region, at least in the summer months. The Northern Sea route, a shipping lane that connects the Atlantic Ocean to the Pacific Ocean above Russia, is 30% shorter than the traditional route through the Suez Canal. Every year, the number of ships that use this route increases, from four in 2010 to 71 in 2013. It's still far smaller than the number of ships that travel through the Suez Canal (more than 170,000 every year), but the number is certain

new Northern
Sea route

traditional Suez
Canal route

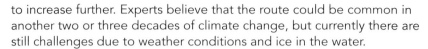

GLOSSARY

legislation (n) a law, or set of laws

observer (n) someone who watches, or is present, but does not have an active role

sustainable (adj) able to continue for a long time because it causes little or no damage

to increase further. Experts believe that the route could be common in another two or three decades of climate change, but currently there are still challenges due to weather conditions and ice in the water.

8 A secondary shipping route is also expected to open up above North America, which would be shorter and faster than the current route through the Panama Canal. The first ship to use this alternative route in 2013 saved several days of voyaging and thus $80,000 in fuel costs.

9 The Arctic Circle is bordered by eight countries: Canada, Denmark, Finland, Iceland, Norway, Russia, Sweden, and the United States. Current laws govern how much of the land, water, and land just beneath the water each country controls. However, as the shape of the area changes, disputes are sure to arise.

10 In 1996, the eight countries that border the Arctic region, together with indigenous people such as the Inuit and the Saami, formed the Arctic Council. This organization sponsors scientific research aimed at sustainable development of the area. So far, the council has passed legislation related to search-and-rescue missions and issues surrounding ocean pollution. Its headquarters are located in Norway, and every two years a different member country is responsible for leading the organization. In 2013, six additional countries—China, India, Italy, Japan, Singapore, and South Korea—became "permanent" members. In addition, 32 other countries have "observer" status. Other international organizations also carry out research in the area. In 2013, the Arctic Council also made a decision to move from influencing policy to making policy. Its primary concerns are the economic and environmental well-being of the area.

11 Plenty of challenges are ahead. One of the largest of these is finances. Without adequate funds, it is difficult to carry out sufficient research and to take needed action. Currently, all of the money spent by the Council comes from voluntary sources.

12 Most people will never visit the Arctic region in their lifetime. However, the health of this remote, sparsely populated region nevertheless affects the health of the entire planet.

D Close reading

Use the annotations you wrote in the margins to quickly help you find this information.

1 What percent of Greenland is currently covered by ice?

2 How many people would be affected by a rise in sea levels?

3 How much of the world's undiscovered petroleum reserves probably lie in the Arctic?

4 What is the name of the new sea route above Russia?

5 How many countries border the Arctic Circle?

6 In what year was the Arctic Council founded?

E Critical thinking

Work in a group. Discuss the questions.

1 Can you think of another situation where climate change made movement easier—or more difficult?

2 Climate change causes some problems, yet also brings some benefits. Should people try to halt or reverse climate change, or let it happen?

3 The Arctic Council is struggling with funding. Where could more money come from? Do you think it's important to fund organizations like this? Why / why not?

Vocabulary development

Verbs for talking about change

1   Categorize the verbs in the box.

demolish   develop   extend   make into
remodel   replace   tear down   transform

To add or add to	To change the shape of	To take away or diminish

2   Choose the correct word to complete each sentence.

1   That old building has been abandoned for years. It should be **extended / torn down**.

2   Building a dam across the river completely **transformed / replaced** the countryside.

3   If the city adds 20 kilometers to the road, it will be necessary to **extend / replace** the sidewalk as well.

4   When I left for college, my parents decided to **make / remodel** my bedroom into a home office.

5   According to this report, there are plans to **develop / demolish** the homes along the river and create a city park instead.

6   If we could **extend / develop** the downtown area further, more businesses would be attracted to the area.

7   The old bridge isn't safe. It has to be **torn down / replaced** with a stronger one.

8   Unfortunately, a new train station design would cost too much money to **demolish / remodel**.

Academic words

1 Match the words in bold with the correct definitions.

1	**abandon** (v)	a	direct; uncomplicated
2	**alternative** (adj)	b	to stop doing something, especially because it is difficult
3	**nevertheless** (adv)		
4	**primary** (adj)	c	very important; first or top priority
5	**purchase** (v)	d	different choice or possibility from among several
6	**straightforward** (adj)		
		e	in spite of that
		f	to buy

2 Complete the paragraph with words from Exercise 1. Change the form if necessary.

When the state government ¹_____ the land, its ²_____ goal was to build railroad tracks through the area so freight trains could transport cargo to the port. Unfortunately, construction of the railroad was not ³_____. Due to the presence of both mountains and swamps, it became too expensive to run a railroad through that area, and two ⁴_____ routes were chosen instead. ⁵_____, even though the original project had to be ⁶_____, the state was able to make good use of the land by turning it into a National Park, where today it is enjoyed by thousands of visitors annually.

3 Work with a partner. Discuss the questions.

1 Think about an investment that your city or country made recently to improve movement and transportation. Was the project straightforward or more complicated? How many alternatives were considered before the decision was made?

2 Talk about a project that you started but had to abandon. What happened? Were you nevertheless able to find an alternative way to meet your goal?

Critical thinking

Claims of fact, value, and policy

Claims are sentences that are used to say whether something is true or false. There must always be some degree of argument. We can divide claims into three types: claims of fact that involve identifying specific problems, claims of value that involve a judgement or evaluation, and claims of policy that involve a solution or series of competing solutions.

Claim of fact

Greenland's ice is melting at increasing rates due to human activity.

Claim of value

The well-being of the Arctic is more important than the mineral resources beneath the ice.

Claim of policy

We should work harder to limit the causes of global warming than on extracting the Arctic's mineral wealth.

1 Read the statements. Decide if they contain *F* (Claims of fact), *V* (Claims of value), or *P* (Claims of policy).

1 The beauty of Yellowstone National Park is beyond question. ___

2 There needs to be a reduction in tourist numbers to ensure the conservation of the National Park. ___

3 The Panama Canal was built to save sailing time for cargo ships. ___

2 Read the statements from Exercise 1 again and match them to the sentences.

a However, it could be argued that military use of the canal was equally important as trade.

b The magnificent mountains and forests create an impressive picture for the visitor.

c If we do not act, then this natural wilderness risks being lost forever.

3 Notice how the type of claim has an effect on what type of statement follows it. Match the type of claim to the type of following statement that can be used to emphasize or analyze it.

1 claim of fact   a a reinforcement to the claim
2 claim of value   b a claim on behalf of another person
3 claim of policy   c a counterclaim

Writing model

You are going to learn about using the future passive and how to organize a comparison essay. You are then going to use these skills to write a short essay comparing two maps.

A Model

Read the essay prompt. Then study the maps. Brainstorm all of the changes that you can see in the maps.

"The two maps show an area now and a development proposal. Summarize the information by selecting and reporting the main features. Make comparisons where relevant."

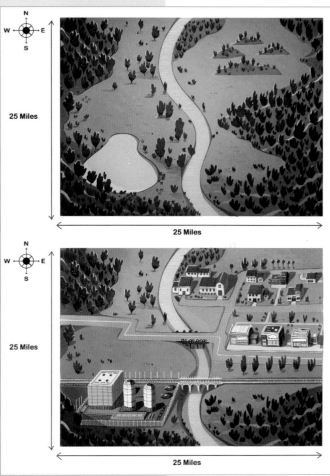

B Analyze

Read the student model and answer the questions.

1 The two maps show the same area of land. The first map shows the area the way it is today, and the second map shows a proposal for development of the area.

2 The area is approximately 25 square miles, and has some hills to the north and a river running through the center. The most noticeable difference is the removal of many trees and natural areas and the construction of transportation systems and buildings.

3 The area is currently a forest. In the development proposal, most trees will be removed. While the river will remain unchanged, a small lake in the southwest will be filled in. Houses will be constructed on some of the open areas as well. Houses and stores will occupy much of the area.

4 In addition, roads and a railroad will be constructed. The main road will run from east to west, and there will be a bridge over the river. A railroad will be built parallel to the road, and a bridge over the river will also be built. There will be houses and other buildings along some of the smaller roads.

1 Which of the paragraphs do these things? Write 1, 2, 3, and 4.

___ summarize the changes   ___ discuss removal of natural features

___ discuss new construction   ___ restate the writing prompt

2 Is there an introduction? Is there a conclusion?

Grammar

Future passive

The passive is used when the object receiving the action is more important than whoever is doing the action. The future passive (*will* + *be* + past participle) is used to describe events that have not happened yet.

Examples:

Some people will construct a bridge.
People will not cut down trees in the park.

*A bridge **will be constructed**.*
*Trees in the park **will not (won't) be cut down**.*

In these examples, we don't know who will be constructing the bridge or cutting the trees. What is important is the bridge and the trees.

1 Complete the sentences with the future passive of the verbs in parentheses.

   1 Under the proposal, the existing swamp area (reduce) _____.

   2 The removal of the swamps means a lot of mosquitos (kill)

      _____.

   3 When the mosquitos are gone, houses for the workers (build)

      _____.

   4 Schedules for the workers (not / plan) _____ until they arrive.

   5 The mountains (demolish) _____ to make room for roads.

   6 It has been decided that the bridge (not / replace) _____.

2 Rewrite the sentences with the future passive.

   1 Some people will remodel our kitchen next year.
      Our kitchen will be remodeled next year.

   2 They will construct a new lock for the canal this month.

      _____

   3 The director will not sign the contract before the meeting.

      _____

   4 We will find additional funding.

      _____

   5 Workers will clear the land.

      _____

   6 They will not charge ships more than $10,000 to use the canal.

      _____

   7 We will hire 200 more workers.

      _____

Writing skill

We use a number of different phrases to avoid overusing *will* in a description of a plan for the future.

These phrases are used to show that we are not certain that these events or actions will actually take place. Make sure you focus on subject-verb agreement when you replace *will* with one of these phrases.

is/are set to   *is/are projected to*
is/are due to   *is/are forecast to*
is/are likely to   *is/are expected to*

We can also use plan in different ways:

plan on **verb** + *-ing* something   *plan to* do something

1 Rewrite these sentences in your notebook with the phrase in parentheses to avoid overusing *will*.

    1 The village will be replaced by a large factory complex. (set)
    2 This change will have happened by the end of 2050. (project)
    3 The population will increase dramatically over the next decade. (likely)
    4 The industrial areas will be demolished in the coming months. (due)
    5 Most of the trees will be removed to allow the construction of new housing. (expect)
    6 The number of malaria cases will probably decrease in the next few years. (forecast)

2 Rewrite these sentences in your notebook with *plan* to avoid overusing *will*.

    1 The government will reduce the amount of parkland in the area. (plan on)
    2 The city will dramatically increase the amount of public transportation in the area by the end of this decade. (plan to)
    3 We will have doubled our profits by the end of this financial quarter. (plan to)
    4 The city will increase the size of its park area within the next few years. (plan on)
    5 The department will make most of its staff take a pay cut. (plan on)

3 Make predictions about changes to the area where you live using the patterns you practiced in Exercises 1 and 2.

Writing task

You are going to write a comparative description in response to the following:
"The two maps show an existing city and proposed changes for the next ten years. Summarize the information by selecting and reporting the main features. Make comparisons where relevant."

Today

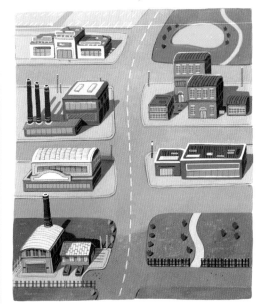

50 square kilometres

Proposal: The next ten years

50 square kilometres

Brainstorm

Make a quick list of changes that you see in the two maps.

Plan

Group the changes in a logical fashion and decide which changes are the most important and will feature in the first paragraph. Use subsequent paragraphs to give more detail about the changes you have selected.

Write

Use your plan to help you write your description. Remember to use the future passive and language to describe future plans. Answer the essay question. Your essay should be about 150–200 words long.

Share

Exchange your essay with a partner. Use the checklist on page 189 to help you provide feedback to your partner.

Rewrite and edit

Consider your partner's comments and write your final draft. Think about:

- whether you described the most important changes
- whether you used the future passive appropriately
- whether you used other language to describe future plans.

Review

Wordlist

MACMILLAN DICTIONARY

Vocabulary preview

arise (v) ***	halt (v) *	toll (n) *
cargo (n) *	indigenous (adj)	treaty (n) **
coastal (adj) **	marine (adj) *	zone (n) **
dispute (n) ***	reef (n) *	

Vocabulary development

demolish (v) *	make into (phr v)	tear down (phr v)
develop (v) ***	remodel (v)	transform (v) **
extend (v) ***	replace (v) ***	

Academic words

abandon (v) **	nevertheless (adv) ***	purchase (v) **
alternative (adj) ***	primary (adj) ***	straightforward (adj) **

Academic words review

Complete the sentences with the words in the box.

alternative	decade	primary	reluctant	straightforward

1 Getting the countries that border the Arctic to agree will be far from
   _____.

2 The research is likely to take at least a _____ to complete.

3 The city council is _____ to reduce the amount of parkland in the
   area.

4 As the sea levels begin to change, _____ shipping routes need to be
   found.

5 At the present time, the spread of malaria is the issue of _____
   concern in this region.

Unit review

Reading 1	☐	I can annotate a text.
Reading 2	☐	I can recognize organization.
Study skill	☐	I can set priorities.
Vocabulary	☐	I can use vocabulary for describing change.
Grammar	☐	I can use the future passive.
Writing	☐	I can compare maps.

6 DISEASE

Discussion point

Discuss with a partner.

1 How important is it to follow the advice in the infographic?

It's incredibly important for a number of reasons like …

2 What should governments do to prevent the spread of diseases?

The most important thing to do is …

3 Should medicine to prevent diseases be given free to those who need it? Why / why not?

The most important thing to do is …

PREVENTING DISEASE

Washing hands regularly is one of the most effective ways to prevent the spread of disease.

Nowadays, immunization can prevent many diseases.

Only use antibiotics when given by a doctor. Always finish the course of drugs.

Stay at home if you vomit, have diarrhea, or have a temperature.

Do not fly, take a train, or take a bus when sick.

Do not eat leftover food that is more than a day old.

VIDEO

MOSQUITO ILLNESSES

Before you watch

Match the words in bold with the correct definitions.

1 **bacteria** (n)
2 **inject** (v)
3 **sterile** (adj)
4 **suppress** (n)

a stop a physical process from happening or developing

b unable to reproduce

c to introduce something into the body using a needle and syringe

d microscopic organisms that can cause disease and decay

UNIT
AIMS

READING 1 Recognizing paragraph structure
READING 2 Identifying sentence functions
STUDY SKILLS Using feedback from your tutors

VOCABULARY Cause and effect
GRAMMAR *unless* and *Provided*
WRITING Cause-and-effect essays

Disinfection workers in the subway, South Korea.

While you watch

Read the sentences then watch the video. Write *T* (True), or *F* (False).

1 The mosquito eggs are injected with bacteria. ___
2 Then the male mosquitos kill the female mosquitos. ___
3 Each researcher can inject 200 eggs with bacteria a day. ___
4 The researchers in Sharzai have reduced the mosquito population by 90%. ___

After you watch

Work with a partner. Discuss the questions.

1 Which of these do you think is more dangerous mosquitos, tigers, or sharks? Justify your opinion.
   I think … because …
2 Do you know any ways to prevent mosquitos from biting?
3 What are the major causes of disease and illness in your country? What can be done to prevent them?
   I think the major causes are …
   We should …

Fighting cholera

A Vocabulary preview

Complete the sentences with the words in the box.

associate　effective　gather　infected　major　polluted　proof　supply

1　There is _____ that shows that the disease is spread through the air.
2　A _____ of fresh water is essential to avoid disease.
3　Many people _____ malaria with long periods of rainfall.
4　_____ air can cause a number of health problems.
5　Antibiotics are the most _____ treatment for the illness.
6　Over 10,000 people were _____ by the disease.
7　Heart disease is a _____ cause of death worldwide.
8　Scientists are trying to _____ data together to test their theory.

B Before you read

Preparing to read

Work with a partner. How many of these diseases have you heard of? What do governments, organizations, and people do to fight the spread of these diseases?

bird flu　cholera　Ebola　heart disease　Zika virus

C Global reading

Predicting

1　These words are taken from each paragraph of *Fighting Cholera*. What do you think the topic of each paragraph is?

　1　paragraph 1 – cholera, diarrhea, dehydration, infected, treatment, die
　　　topic: _____
　2　paragraph 2 – outbreaks, started, transported, waste
　　　topic: _____
　3　paragraph 3 – thought, theory
　　　topic: _____
　4　paragraph 4 – transmitted, fresh water, drinking, waste
　　　topic: _____
　5　paragraph 5 – outbreaks, water, not affected, not infected, evidence, stop
　　　topic: _____
　6　paragraph 6 – sewer system … built, propose … theory, accepted
　　　topic: _____

2　Read the text and check your predictions.

GLOSSARY

outbreak (n) the sudden start of war, disease, violence etc

sewer (n) an underground pipe or passage that carries sewage

Fighting cholera

1 Cholera is a disease that is transmitted by drinking water contaminated with bacteria. It leads to diarrhea, which can result in high levels of dehydration. Today, according to the World Health Organization, around three to five million people are infected with cholera. These days the disease can successfully be treated provided that drinking water with added salt is consumed. As a result of this cheap and effective treatment, most people survive. However, the number of people that die from cholera still exceeds 100,000 every year.

2 Around the world there have been many outbreaks of cholera that have killed millions of people. During the first industrial revolution, the disease started to become an even bigger killer. Transported between major towns and cities by people buying and selling goods, once the disease reached a new area many people were quickly infected, and it caused many pandemics. A pandemic is an outbreak of a disease that rapidly leads to large numbers of people being affected. As more and more people moved to cities, the infrastructure of many places did not undergo a development process at the required rate. Sewers were not built quickly enough to take human waste away, and many major rivers and other sources of water became polluted.

3 In the early days, most people thought that cholera was spread through polluted air. Known as the miasma theory, the visible effects of heavy industry understandably led people to suspect that bad air was the cause of the pandemic. The actual cause of the spread of infectious diseases—germ theory—was not yet known. This theory, suggested by Louis Pasteur, argued that small organisms, too small to see with the human eye, grow and reproduce on people, plants, and animals. However, one local doctor, John Snow, was not convinced that this was how cholera spread.

4 Snow felt that provided cholera was a disease transmitted through the air, then it would affect people's lungs. However, it had no impact on people's breathing. Instead, it attacked people's bowels and caused very bad diarrhea. At this time in London,

people did not receive a fresh water supply to their homes. They took their drinking water from the river Thames, which was also where sewage was deposited. Essentially, people were drinking their own waste. Snow proposed that cholera was actually a disease transmitted through water rather than air. Initially, unless he could gather proof, his theory was unlikely to be accepted.

5 Snow went door to door mapping out where the main outbreaks occurred. This method led him to a young child, Frances Lewis. John discovered that the mother had washed Frances' soiled clothes in a nearby cesspool, used to store human waste. Unknown at the time, this cesspool had been leaking into the main local fresh water supply, polluting it. This simple action was the cause of the outbreak of cholera in the Broad Street area. At the same time, a local workhouse with over 500 employees was not affected. Only five people working there had died. Snow believed this was because the workhouse had its own fresh-water pump that was not infected. With this and other evidence, he was able to persuade the local government to close the Broad Street pump and arguably stop the pandemic.

6 Although Snow now had significant evidence to support his theory, it was still not widely accepted. Many people, including doctors, still believed the water in the Thames was fresh enough to drink. In 1858, John Snow died. Later that summer, the hot weather caused the smell of the river Thames to become so bad that politicians were nearly forced to leave the Houses of Parliament. As a result, a huge sewer system was built beneath London to give people access to clean water. However, nearly a decade later, in the last area to get access to the sewer system there was another cholera outbreak. Henry Whitehead, a researcher who worked with John Snow, used this evidence and the previous examples they had gathered to propose the theory again. Finally, the theory was accepted. John Snow's words to Henry Whitehead had come true: "You and I may not live to see the day, and my name may be forgotten when it comes, but the time will arrive when great outbreaks of cholera will be things of the past; and it is the knowledge of the way in which the disease is propagated which will cause them to disappear."

Recognizing paragraph structure

D Close reading

Texts sometimes have one overall structure such as cause and effect, problem and solution, etc. However, texts also often have paragraphs within them with particular structures. For example, one paragraph may describe an event and another may define a key term. Also paragraphs themselves will often have sentences with particular functions and structures.

1 Read the first paragraph in *Fighting cholera*. Match each sentence in the paragraph to these functions.

  A   Describing the effects of cholera   ____
  B   Describing the effects of treatment   ____
  C   Describing the treatment   ____
  D   Explaining the cause of cholera   ____
  E   Describing the effects of not treating it   ____
  F   Describing cholera today   ____

2 Read the rest of the text. Underline the sentences with these functions.

  A   paragraph 2 — defining a major situation
  B   paragraph 3 — the cause of cholera
  C   paragraph 4 — the effects of cholera
  D   paragraph 5 — the effects of the investigation
  E   paragraph 6 — the effect of a smelly river Thames

E Critical thinking

Work in a group. Discuss the questions.

1 Why do you think lots of people did not believe John Snow?

  They perhaps didn't believe him because …

2 Think about research you read every day, for example, the effects of a diet. Do you always believe the research? Why / why not?

  I usually / don't usually believe it because …

  It depends. I sometimes believe it when …

Study skills | Using feedback from your tutors

Read through your work and the tutor's comments. Be constructive. Keep asking yourself, "How can this help me improve my work?"

After each comment, check whether you understand what it was that made the tutor write it. Highlight any comments that you feel are useful to you for your next piece of work.

Create a table or divide a page into sections to show major issues, areas that lose a lot of marks, and minor errors.

© Stella Cottrell (2013)

1   Match the comments to the marking criteria. Then divide the issues into major, or minor.

1	Evidence and research	40%	_____
2	Critical thinking	30%	_____
3	Organization and structure	10%	_____
4	Spelling, grammar, and vocabulary	10%	_____
5	Bibliography	10%	_____

a   *You have failed to answer the question asked.*

b   *While you present convincing arguments, your essay is let down by a lack of research.*

c   *Unfortunately, you simply describe the theory. The question requires you to <u>evaluate</u> the theory.*

d   *The essay is well researched, but very hard to follow due to the organization.*

e   *There are a number of spelling errors throughout.*

f   *You have included a bibliography, but you haven't used the correct method.*

2   Look at the marking criteria used to mark one of your essays. Read the feedback from your teacher and divide the comments into major and minor issues.

3   Compare your notes with a partner. Discuss your priorities for improving your work.

The economic impact of disease

A Vocabulary preview

1 Complete the questions with the words in the box. Change the form if necessary.

alarm	dependent	distinguish	doubtful
overall	overlook	productive	related

1 Are you ever _____ when you hear about diseases around the world?

2 What impact might disease or illness have on a country's _____?

3 Which consequences of illness do you think are often _____?

4 How easy is it to _____ between the impact of diseases and other world events on tourism?

5 How is lifestyle _____ to the increase of diseases?

6 _____, deaths from infectious diseases are falling. Why?

7 How _____ are you that scientists will ever find a cure to all forms of cancer?

8 The world is often _____ on companies to develop drugs. Why might this be a problem?

2 Work with a partner. Discuss the questions in Exercise 1.

B Before you read

Predicting

Look at the pictures and the title. How might disease be connected to the economy of a country? Work with a partner and try to think of three possible connections.

Infectious diseases may reduce the number of tourists in a country, which means that …

C Global reading

Identifying main ideas

Read *The economic impact of disease* and match the topics (A–F) to paragraphs (2–7).

A The effect on medical services ____

B The impact of non-infectious diseases ____

C The effect of time off work ____

D How the travel industry can be affected ____

E The loss of many lives ____

F The impact of infectious diseases ____

The economic impact *of disease*

1 No one would question how catastrophic the impact of diseases can be on society. Loss of life is clearly the biggest impact, however, something less often spoken about is the economic impact disease can have on society. In fact, illness not only has a significant effect on a single domestic economy, but it may even affect world economy. From the simple loss of productivity, due to days off sick, through to the long-term impact on regional tourism, there are many widespread economic consequences of disease.

2 On a simplistic level, a country's economic output diminishes due to the number of productive days lost from the impact of diseases and illnesses. It is virtually impossible to say precisely which diseases and illnesses have the most significant economic impact. However, millions of days are lost each year due to health-related issues. From stress, through to muscular injuries and serious long-term illnesses, a country can lose billions of dollars of revenue.

3 Of course, the loss of working days is one sole economic impact. Additionally, there is the economic effect on health services. Unless all health care is private, this is ultimately provided by taxes paid to the government. Hence, any increase in the usage of doctors, accident and emergency or pharmaceutical purchases, is a direct economic cost to the wider society. While it is doubtful this will lead to increased taxation, it could result in less expenditure on other areas such as education, transportation, or social support.

4 It is important though to distinguish between economic losses as a consequence of illnesses or injuries and those related to diseases. Diseases can predominantly be grouped into two categories—infectious and non-infectious. An infectious disease is one which can be passed from one person to another. When we consider infectious diseases that emerge such as Ebola, SARS, and various forms of the flu, they are initially not well known, and there can be widespread alarm in society. Furthermore, a new disease has the considerable cost of developing a new vaccine. It is estimated that to develop a new vaccine costs in the region of $200 to $500 million dollars. Additionally, unless it is well managed, it can also result in panic and the closure of public services such as schools. Other events that require police or medical presences, such as sporting events or public celebrations, may have to be canceled or postponed. All of which has an economic cost.

5 Furthermore, when an infectious disease breaks out in an area, it can have detrimental consequences on the local tourism industry. When SARS, a breathing-related illness, broke out in South-East Asia it was estimated to have cost millions of jobs. At its peak, some countries' tourism sectors collapsed by 50% on the previous year. Even areas not affected by the disease saw a drop in tourism as people became concerned about the spread of SARS and fearful of flying in general. However, merely 8,000 people were affected by SARS and this resulted in barely 800 deaths. When you consider that the number of deaths from malaria exceeds 400,000 people annually, the number of people affected by SARS was miniscule. However, the economic impact, as a consequence of people's fears, was estimated to be millions of dollars.

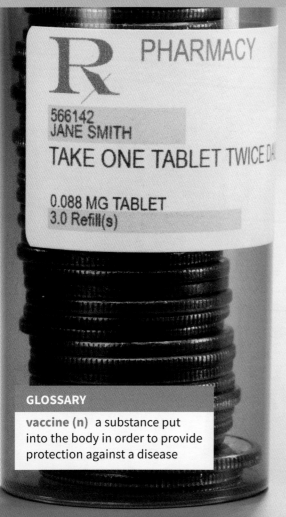

GLOSSARY

vaccine (n) a substance put into the body in order to provide protection against a disease

6 Commonly known diseases are another factor to take into account when considering the effect and cost of fighting diseases. This is especially true in relation to non-infectious diseases. Worldwide, governments have implemented various methods to reduce smoking rates. From public bans to media campaigns, governments have tried to wipe out the economic burden of smoking. One such campaign, in the U.K., was the "Stoptober" event. This media campaign encouraged smokers to try to give up smoking during the month of October. In this month, it was thought an additional 350,000 people attempted to give up smoking. The economic benefits for a country can be vast. Early deaths, medical treatment, and lost working days' account for billions of dollars in economic costs.

7 In the worst cases, exposure to a disease can have a significant impact on the population as a whole. Some diseases have reduced individual countries' populations by as much as 20%. One disease that affected the world by causing a fall of up to 5% in the population, was the flu of 1918, sometimes known as the Spanish flu. The average life expectancy dropped by about 12 years and as many as 100 million people died. The flu usually affects the elderly and young much more than healthy adults, but this flu had a detrimental effect on those that were healthy too. As a result, the world lost a vast proportion of its working population. To a large extent, the elderly and young are dependent on this group for economic support. Households may simply have had less income, and government tax revenue would have been reduced. A disease like this has immediate and long-term economic consequences across all parts of society.

8 While the health effects and the tragic loss of life are clearly the most significant factors when we discuss diseases, the economic consequences cannot be overlooked. It places pressure on all areas of society, from healthcare to education to the overall demography of society. Illnesses and diseases are perhaps one of the single biggest causes of a weaker economy around the world.

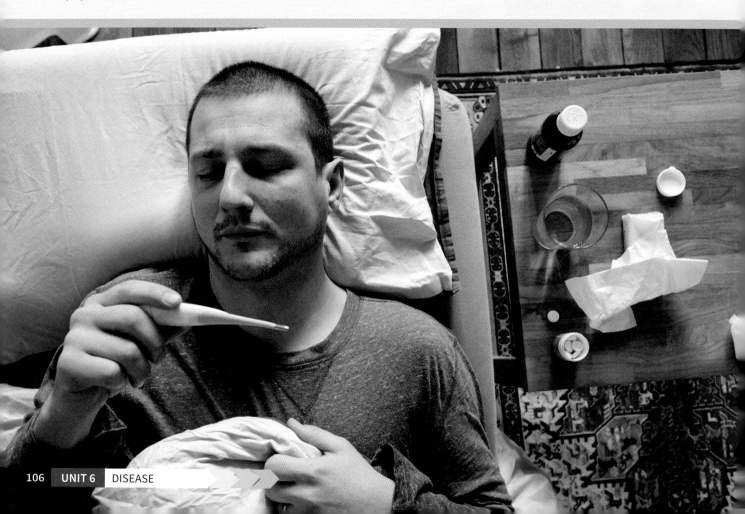

D Close reading

> Identifying the functions of a sentence can help you to understand the purpose of the writer and the organization of a text. Functions include **defining**, **speculating**, **classifying**, **reporting**, and **naming**.
>
> **Defining:** *A pandemic is an outbreak of a disease that rapidly leads to large numbers of people being affected.*
>
> **Speculating:** *While it is doubtful this will lead to increased taxation, it could result in less expenditure in other areas.*
>
> **Classifying:** *Pain can usually be categorized into two types: chronic or acute.*
>
> **Reporting:** *Today, according to the World Health Organization, around three to five million people are infected with cholera.*
>
> **Naming:** *One disease that affected the world by causing a fall of up to 5% in the population, was the flu of 1918, sometimes known as the Spanish flu.*

Read the sentences and match them to the functions from the *Identifying sentence functions* box.

1   When SARS, a breathing related illness, broke out in South-East Asia it was estimated to have cost millions of jobs. _____

2   One such campaign in the UK was the "Stoptober" event. _____

3   An infectious disease is one that can be passed from one person to another. _____

4   Illnesses and diseases are perhaps one of the single biggest causes of a weaker economy around the world. _____

5   Diseases can predominantly be grouped into two categories—infectious and non-infectious. _____

E Critical thinking

Work in a group. Discuss the questions.

1   Why do you think people rarely talk about the economic effects of diseases?
    Probably, because …

2   Which of the economic impacts described in the text do you think is the worst? Why?
    … is almost certainly the worst because …

Vocabulary development

Cause and effect

We use a number of different words and expressions to show cause and effect. Some words place the cause first and the effect second, and others place the effect first and the cause second. For example:

      cause   effect

*Unclean water can **result in** an increase in diseases.*

      effect   cause

*Diseases such as typhoid are **caused by** unclean water.*

1   Underline the cause and circle the effect in each of these sentences.

   1   Many days can be taken off sick. As a result, companies may lose income.

   2   In the worst cases, a lower birth rate can result from a sharp rise in an infectious disease.

   3   Lifestyle choices can result in an increase in many diseases.

   4   The world's population fell by 5% because of the 1918 flu.

   5   People often fear a breakout of a new disease. Therefore, governments need to communicate their effects quickly.

   6   A sharp increase in the levels of any disease can place pressure on the medical profession. Consequently, many governments have emergency plans to help deal with this.

2   Choose the correct word or phrase to complete each sentence.

   1   The outbreak **resulted in / as a result** a fall in tourism.

   2   Diseases can have significant economic impacts. **Consequently, / Because of,** countries need to fund research into diseases.

   3   More days being taken off work **therefore / resulted from** increased levels of depression and stress.

   4   Governments have a responsibility for the welfare of their residents. **Therefore, / Because of,** they should develop vaccines that fight dangerous diseases.

   5   **Consequently / Because of** lost working days, the government's income from taxes fell.

   6   The government reduced funding for disease research. **As a result, / Result in,** fewer cures are being discovered.

3   Work with a partner. What are the major causes of falls and rises in diseases in the last 50 years? What have been the effects of these changes?

Academic words

1 Match the words in bold with the correct definitions.

1 **collapse** (v)
2 **exposure** (n)
3 **hence** (adv)
4 **transmission** (n)
5 **ultimately** (adv)
6 **undergo** (v)
7 **virtually** (adv)
8 **widespread** (adj)

a the state of being put into a situation in which something harmful or dangerous might affect you

b used to emphasize the main point you are speaking about

c to fall dramatically

d used to emphasize that a statement is almost completely true

e used for introducing something that is a result of the fact that has just been stated

f a process by which a disease spreads from one person to another

g happening or existing in many places, or affecting many people

h to experience something, especially something that is unpleasant but necessary

2 Complete the sentences with words from Exercise 1.

1 _____ all diseases will have a cure in the next 100 years, but not all.

2 _____, most deaths in rich countries could be prevented with lifestyle changes.

3 If we discontinued public funding, the research industry would _____.

4 Hospitals should _____ infection control audits to limit the spread of diseases.

5 Diseases are mainly spread by individuals. _____, it is the individual's responsibility, not the government's, to prevent their spread.

6 _____ to a disease, such as Ebola, can be fatal. Therefore governments should place restrictions on travel.

7 The residents of a local community are responsible for preventing the _____ of diseases such as the flu.

8 Many diseases have become more _____ due to international travel.

3 Check (✓) the sentences you agree with in Exercise 2. Compare your opinions with a partner.

Critical thinking

Evaluating evidence

It is important that any evidence you use directly and logically supports the point you want to make. A vague or loose connection is not enough. The data should also be sufficient enough to support the claim being made. In other words, you should not make generalizations above and beyond the data without sufficiently hedging your opinion.

> Workplace illnesses are one of the major factors affecting company profitability throughout the world and ultimately lead to a huge loss of income. In one survey of 200 leading European companies, it was estimated that on average each person takes six days off sick each year. For a company of 2,000 employees, this is 12,000 lost working days.

1 Read the *Evaluating evidence* box. Then read the first sentence of the example paragraph again and answer the questions.

  1 Does the data in the paragraph strongly support this opinion?

  2 Is the data sufficient enough?

2 Read the following evidence. Which statements could possibly be used to support the essay question: *"How important is it for countries to fund research into disease?"*

  1 Countries with high investment into disease prevention research have lower rates of most diseases.

  2 Companies spend the most money researching drugs that will be the most profitable.

  3 It is estimated that cancer costs the U.K. alone nearly £20 billion annually, of which £5 billion is directly in national healthcare costs.

3 Work with a partner. Discuss the questions.

  1 How can you decide whether evidence is sufficient enough to support your point?

  2 How can you eliminate irrelevant information?

  3 What is the weakness in making generalizations beyond the data?

Writing model

You are going to learn about using *provided* and *unless*, and including definitions in your writing. You are then going to use these skills to write a cause-and-effect essay about funding research into disease.

A Analyze

Read the essay question and use the brainstorm below to complete the model essay.

"How important is it to teach children about how diseases are transmitted?"

Effects of hand washing	Effects of vaccination
Provided good hygiene is established at a young age, it can be effective in reducing the breakout of a disease.	However, as a result of vaccination, this number was reduced to just a few hundred within 20 years.
Unless children do this before eating, they have a significantly increased chance of being infected.	Many diseases, unless prevented by a vaccine, can potentially lead to a loss of life.

B Model

While much research funding focuses on developing cures for infectious diseases, one of the most effective tools is educating people to stop the transmission of a disease. This is particularly true when considering young children. Provided these techniques are taught at a young age, the spread of these diseases could be significantly reduced.

The spread of many diseases can be reduced simply by educating children to regularly wash their hands. [1]_____ When children develop poor hand-washing methods, it can lead to diseases such as the flu, and other illnesses such as diarrhea, becoming widespread. [2]_____

Another technique, which affects both children and parents, is that of the importance of vaccines. [3]_____ Polio is an infectious disease that destroys muscles. In 1985 over 400,000 people were infected with polio. [4]_____

Education is key in disease prevention. The education of everyone is important, however, developing children's knowledge and habits could ultimately lead to significant reductions in long-term disease break out.

Discuss the questions with a partner.

1 Do you think educating children about things such as hand washing is effective?

2 Do you think governments should spend money on programs educating people about diseases?

3 Who should be responsible for funding research into diseases?

Grammar

Unless and *provided*

Unless

Unless means "except if" or "only if"

Initially, **unless** *he could gather proof, his theory was unlikely to be accepted.*
= His theory would be accepted only if he could get proof.

Furthermore, **unless** *it is well managed, it could also result in panic and the closure of public services such as schools.*
= except if it is well managed, panic may occur and schools could close

Provided

Provided means "if" or "on condition that"

Today, the disease can largely be fought **provided** *drinking water with added salt is consumed.*
= If water and salt are consumed, the disease can be fought.

1 Choose the correct word to complete each sentence.

1 **Provided / Unless** the media react in a calm way, people tend not to panic.

2 **Unless / Provided** people are educated about the importance of vaccination, they may not accept it.

3 **Provided / Unless** people wash their hands, the spread of diseases can be reduced.

4 **Unless / Provided** more funding is made available, a cure is unlikely to be found.

5 **Unless / Provided** all children have the vaccine, the risk an outbreak is very low.

6 **Unless / Provided** infected people follow the advice to stay at home, the outbreak should be controlled.

2 Rewrite the sentences with the same meaning. Use *unless* in your sentence.

1 People need to listen carefully or they won't know what to do.

2 Governments must act soon or there might be a pandemic.

3 It is a holiday today. Doctors will only see people for an emergency.

4 You're not allowed in. Only relatives can come in.

Writing skill

> Definitions are usually written using two structures. One is a noun + a prepositional phrase:
>
> **This kind of vaccination** and other medicines *can be used for fighting diseases.*
>
> **Word being defined**   category   *use/detail*
>
> Or a relative clause:
>
> **A pandemic** is an outbreak of a disease *that rapidly leads to large numbers of people being affected.*
>
> **Word being defined**   category   *use/detail*

1   Read the sentences and identify
   a   the word being defined.
   b   the category.
   c   the use or detail.

   1   The flu is a contagious illness transmitted between individuals.
   2   Quarantine is a secure place for putting infected people in isolation.
   3   A campaign is a series of organized events for raising awareness of and protesting against an issue.

2   Reorder the words to make sentences.

   1   is an infectious disease / transmitted by consuming contaminated water / Typhoid
   2   that are made up of one tiny cell / bacteria / are small living organisms
   3   that protects you from contracting diseases / the immune system / is a complex system within the body

3   Write definitions for the following words.

   1   medicine   _____
   2   non-infectious disease _____
   3   evidence   _____
   4   researcher   _____

Writing task

You are going to write a cause-and-effect essay in response to the following:
"How important is it for countries to fund research into disease?"

Brainstorm

Complete the brainstorm below with your ideas.

Plan

1 Do you think it is important for countries to fund disease research?

2 What are the effects of funding disease research?

3 What are the effects of not funding disease research?

Write

Use your plan to help you write your essay. Remember to use *provided* and *unless* to talk about conditions where appropriate, and to use language of cause and effect. Your text should be 250 words long.

Share

Exchange your essay with a partner. Use the checklist on page 189 to help you provide feedback to your partner.

Rewrite and edit

Consider your partner's comments and write your final draft. Think about:

- whether you structured your essay clearly
- whether you used *unless* and *provided* appropriately
- whether you used language of cause and effect appropriately.

Review

Wordlist

MACMILLAN DICTIONARY

Vocabulary preview

alarm (n) **	gather (v) ***	productive (adj) **
associate (v) ***	infected (adj)	proof (n) **
dependent (adj) ***	major (adj) ***	related (adj) **
distinguish (v) ***	overall (adv) **	supply (n) ***
doubtful (adj) **	overlook (v) **	
effective (adj) ***	polluted (adj)	

Vocabulary development

as a result (phrase)	consequently (adv) **	result in (phrase)
because of (phrase)	result from (phrase)	therefore (adv) ***

Academic words

collapse (v) **	transmission (n) **	virtually (adv) ***
exposure (n) **	ultimately (adv) **	widespread (adj) **
hence (adv) ***	undergo (v) **	

Academic words review

Complete the sentences with the words in the box.

collapse	hence	nevertheless	undergo	widespread

1   A new vaccine has caused the number of new infections to _____.
2   The disease was not well known to scientists. _____, it was to have an enormous impact on the population.
3   The disease was highly infectious, _____ the panic among the local community.
4   There was _____ alarm when news of the disease spread.
5   Everyone in my company has to _____ a health check.

Unit review

Reading 1	☐	I can recognize text organization.
Reading 2	☐	I can identify sentence functions.
Vocabulary	☐	I can use words and expressions to show cause and effect.
Study skill	☐	I can use feedback from my tutors.
Grammar	☐	I can use *unless* and *provided*.
Writing	☐	I can write cause-and-effect essays.

The longest surviving things in the world

There are nearly **half a million people** worldwide **over the age of 100.** Many believe **diet** and **exercise** to be the main reasons for their age.

Bristlecone trees—the oldest trees in the world are **over 5,000 years old.** They survive so long because almost nothing else can live in the **difficult conditions.** They **survive drought and disease** like no other plant.

Greenland sharks can live to **400 years old.** They survive by **eating anything.** Also, nothing eats them because their flesh is **poisonous.**

Giant tortoise—the only land animal to live **more than 200 years.** Its **shell protects** it from predators. It also uses energy very **slowly.**

No one can agree on the **oldest** continuously inhabited **city in the world,** but nearly all are in the **Middle East** or **Mediterranean.**

Discussion point

Discuss with a partner.

1 Who is the oldest person you know? Why do you think they have lived so long?

The oldest person is …
They have probably lived so long because …

2 Why do you think some places have survived so long?

They might have survived so long because …

3 Is it important to protect ancient places or things under threat?

Yes, I think so because …
No, I don't think so because …

VIDEO

WATER POLLUTION

Before you watch

Match the words in bold with their synonyms.

1 **absorb** (v)   a kinds
2 **factor** (n)   b turn back
3 **reverse** (v)   c element
4 **settlement** (n)   d city
5 **species** (n)   e take in

UNIT AIMS

READING 1 Identifying support for opinions
READING 2 Using research questions
STUDY SKILL Avoiding self-sabotage

VOCABULARY Describing graphs
GRAMMAR Present perfect progressive
WRITING Inferring the meaning of data in graphs

Bristlecone tree on a starry night.

While you watch

Complete the summary of the video. Write one word in each blank.

Lake Titicaca is the biggest lake in ¹_____ America. Its water is polluted by the nearby ²_____ called El Alto. As a result, local families find it hard to survive and many people ³_____ to other countries.

The people cannot continue farming or ⁴_____ if the water is too polluted. Fortunately, experts think it's not too late to ⁵_____ the process of pollution.

After you watch

Work with a partner. Discuss the questions.

1 Is there an area in your country that is similar to Lake Titicaca?

No, there isn't. / Yes, there is. It's called …

2 Do you know of any places that have faced problems like the ones in the video?

One such place could be …

3 Do you think Esteban's situation is a serious issue? Why / why not?

I think / I don't think it's a serious issue because …

The death of languages

A Vocabulary preview

1 Complete the sentences with the words in the box.

> commerce   minority   nation   official
> ruling   superior   urbanization   widely

1 English is the most _____ spoken language because it is the language of business.

2 No language is _____ to another. All languages are equal.

3 _____ happens because people can get better jobs in cities.

4 _____ languages need to be protected in order to survive.

5 _____ groups and leaders should respect the rights and wishes of smaller groups.

6 A language gains an _____ position when it is recognized as the language of law and politics.

7 _____ affects many decisions. The majority of people are focused on economic success.

8 One _____ does not have to have a single language or culture. It can have a wide range of cultures.

2 Check (✓) the sentences you agree with. Compare your choices with a partner.

B Before you read

Predicting

Before you read *The death of languages*, discuss the questions with a partner.

1 How many languages do you think are spoken in the world?

2 Which parts of the world have the greatest variety of languages?

3 What are the five most spoken languages?

C Global reading

Reading for main ideas

Read the questions and choose the paragraphs in the text that contain the answers.

A Why do some languages become more widely used than others? ___ ___

B Where are a lot of different languages mostly spoken? ___

C What is lost when a language dies? ___

D What are some examples of common languages in the world? ___

E What can be done to protect a language? ___

The death of languages

1 Worldwide there are approximately 7,000 languages spoken today. With around seven billion people in the world, this could mean that each language is spoken by 100,000 people. However, some languages are used much more than others. Half of the world speaks just a small number of languages, with the top five being Mandarin, Spanish, Hindi, English, and Arabic. Together these languages account for just under two billion people in the world. With so many people speaking so few languages, many others are under threat of disappearing. Some estimates suggest that between 50% to 90% of languages will no longer exist by the year 2100. Can and should something be done to stop the death of these languages?

2 The distribution of language diversity varies greatly across the world. For example, there are just over 200 languages spoken in Europe, but around 2,000 in Asia. Some places have an especially high range of local languages. For example, Papua New Guinea is one of the most linguistically diverse countries in the world, with over 800 languages. The problem occurs when fewer and fewer people speak a language. In North America, for example, there are over 150 languages. However, around half of these are spoken by only a small number of people. In fact, around 25% of the world's languages are in a similar situation. Some argue that languages are disappearing as fast as many species of animal. Languages, though, unlike animals are not dependent on surviving in a particular environment, so why are so many disappearing?

3 Some languages die and others become widely used for a variety of reasons. Some are historical and relate to when a small number of nations and their languages spread to different parts of the world. Some languages faced discrimination and were even banned. Others were still used, but because powerful groups preferred a different language, they became less common. Once a language achieves a superior position in society, because it is either enforced through law, or has a special status in education, it makes it hard for other languages to survive. However, historically, and even today, arguably the main reason for the death of a language is commerce.

4 When we think of languages taking over others in commerce, it is easy to quickly jump to the conclusion that the world has become more global. However, this process started along with urbanization as more people moved to cities in search of work and there became a need for common languages. Usually, the one that would emerge as the most common language would be the one associated with strong, often international, economies that people wanted to trade with. Historically, the strength of the British economy around the world meant more people were speaking English. More recently, the economic power of the U.S.A. has continued to push the status of the English language. This has led to the rise of English as a global language. In such a situation where just a few languages come to dominate, should we worry about the survival of other languages?

5 Some argue that losing a language is to lose more than simply its words, grammar, and pronunciation. With it, we lose cultural knowledge and identity. To protect the language, it needs to be given a special status within a society. If there is no need to use a language, or people have little opportunity to use it, then it will ultimately stop existing. Some languages already have so few speakers that the aim now is simply to record the languages before the last speakers die. However, for minority languages with more speakers, there is much that can be done to enable their survival.

6 During the Industrial Revolution, many English speakers moved to Wales and rarely learned Welsh. As a result, living amongst two languages became normal. Between 1891 and 1961, the percentage of Welsh speakers fell from just under 50% to 26% and, by the 1960s, many considered the Welsh language to be under threat. Consequently, The Welsh Language Society was founded to protect the language. Due to its campaigning, and the actions of other groups, Welsh has re-established itself and was granted the status of an official language. Education, from nursery to college, is available in Welsh. Dedicated Welsh TV channels are also broadcast. Most importantly, the trend of decline has reversed and nearly 80% of the population now report being able to speak, read, and write in Welsh.

7 Languages are dying out more rapidly than ever before. However, this does not mean death is certain. With the right support, it is possible for languages that are under threat to survive.

GLOSSARY

trade (v) to buy or sell goods or services

Identifying support for opinions

D Close reading

When you write an essay, you will often want to express your own opinion. However, most academic subjects will require that you also find evidence to support your opinions. It is a good idea to read for reasons, examples, and data because these can provide strong support for your own opinions. It's important that this evidence is relevant and sufficient.

1 Read *The death of languages* again. Underline the sentence or sentences in the text that support these main arguments in a student essay.

   1 Many languages are now spoken by only a few people.

   2 Giving a language a particular legal status can cause the decline of other languages.

   3 The rise of English was once connected to the British, but now they are not as important.

   4 For a language to survive, it needs to be integrated into schools and the media.

2 Read the main argument a student wants to present in their essay. Choose the sentence that best supports her opinion.

Student A believes there are likely to be fewer languages in the future.

   1 In North America, for example, there are over 150 languages. However, around half of these are spoken by only a small number of people.

   2 Languages are dying out more rapidly than ever before. However, this does not mean death is certain.

   3 Some estimates suggest that between 50% to 90% of languages will no longer exist by the year 2100.

E Critical thinking

Work in a group. Discuss the questions.

1 Will the world eventually speak just a small number of languages? Why / why not?

Probably, because …

No, it's not likely because …

2 Why do you think people believe it is important to protect endangered languages?

I think they believe it's important because …

Study skills | Avoiding self-sabotage

It can sometimes be hard to accept that we may not achieve our goals. Many people have set patterns that they use in their daily life to sabotage their own best-laid plans. Examples include:

Not turning up to lectures

Leaving work to the last minute and then missing the deadline

Filling their time with any activity except study

Ask yourself:

What kinds of self-sabotage are you likely to engage in?

How could you recognize self-sabotage?

Is there anybody you trust to point this out to you?

© Stella Cottrell (2013)

GLOSSARY

sabotage (n) things that are done to stop someone from achieving something or to prevent something from being successful

1 Read about this student's experience in a class and discuss the questions that follow.

I signed up for the class in app development not because I particularly like IT, but because I thought developing apps could help my future plans for a business. My major is business and management, so I had assumed the class wouldn't be very technical, but it was. I didn't really understand the first few lectures, so I missed the following seminars because I didn't want to discuss the topics. Our assessment was a presentation, but the other students were so much better than me because I didn't ever meet them to work on the talk. In the end, I failed the class.

1 What mistake did he make before the course started?

2 What mistakes did he make during the course?

2 Work with a partner. Discuss the questions.

1 Do you think you ever self-sabotage?

2 Is there anyone you know well who could see this and point it out to you?

3 How could you stop this behavior from occurring?

3 Work with a partner. Which of the techniques below do you think would help you avoid self-sabotaging?

- setting huge goals
- focusing on your expectations
- breaking tasks down into manageable mini-tasks
- keeping note of your achievements
- reflecting on your failures
- aiming to do a little more with each task you set yourself

More than just survival

A Vocabulary preview

1 Complete the questions with the words in the box.

breed   die out   disrupt   food chain   habitat   shortages   threat   thrive

1 What human activities _____ the environment the most?

2 What can be done to reduce food _____?

3 What animals _____ in your country? Why do they do so well?

4 Some people argue it is natural for animals to _____ because they cannot survive the modern world. Do you agree?

5 Should animals be hunted to protect a _____ or ecosystem?

6 Which _____ is best for wildlife in your country: mountains, desert, jungle, or something else?

7 Should people _____ dogs to be more aggressive?

8 What _____ to the planet do you think is the most worrying?

2 Work with a partner. Discuss the questions in Exercise 1.

B Before you read

Predicting

Look at the images and the title of the reading. What is the text about?

C Global reading

Using research questions

When you are given an essay, it is a good idea to plan research questions to help you focus your reading. These questions should help you to answer part of your essay.

Read the research questions. Match the questions (A–G) to the paragraph of the text (1–7) that contains the information.

A Are scientists discovering other benefits to protecting species?   ____

B What effects does protecting the environment have on the economy?   ____

C How many species become extinct annually?   ____

D What are the main human activities that affect animal numbers?   ____

E What effect can protecting animals have on the food chain?   ____

F What are the risks associated with low species numbers?   ____

G What else do we need to protect an endangered species?   ____

MORE THAN JUST SURVIVAL

1 No one really knows how many species of animal there are in the world, but one estimate puts it at just under nine million. However, the majority of species have not been identified, and we are still discovering new ones at a rapid rate. Since we have identified so few animals, it is difficult to determine the rate of extinction. However, it is thought that between 0.01% and 0.1% of all species could become extinct every year. This rate would mean between 900 and 9,000 extinctions every year. While this is an alarming rate, it is not inevitable that an animal will become extinct. In fact, a number of animals that were close to dying out have actually been brought back from the edge of extinction. Doing so may help humans survive as nature still provides the vast majority of medicines people use.

2 There are a number of different factors that lead to the extinction or near extinction of an animal, including hunting and habitat destruction. An example of this is the gray whale, of which there were once three main groups spread across the world's oceans. One has been hunted to extinction, but two continue to survive. Of these, one is thought to be endangered while the other is thriving. Twice hunted to near extinction, the gray whale was given protected status nearly 80 years ago, and hunting was limited to fewer than 200 annually. In the 1940s, the population had been hunted to fewer than 2,000. However, by the 1990s, the population had risen again to over 23,000. The increasing human population, set to peak at around nine billion, is also threatening the survival of some species. Habitat destruction for resources and farming land has all but wiped out some species such as lemurs and orangutans.

3 When a population falls to such low numbers, or it is confined to a small protected area, this places a number of other challenges on its long-term survival. One big risk is that when animals breed from low numbers, there is not enough variety in their genes. Animals thrive by being diverse, and when animals breed from such a tiny group, there can be dangers of weaknesses developing and animals being unable to survive. The Arabian gazelle was once in decline, but due to protection efforts, its numbers are rapidly increasing again. To reduce the problem of a limited gene pool, the environment agency studied the variation within the species in different areas. The aim was to not just manage the quantity of the population, but also the quality, by trying to increase the variation in genes. A strong and varied DNA pool will make the species' chances of survival much greater.

4 It is important that protection efforts do not just focus on a single species. Protecting the wider food chain can help increase the population of an endangered species. The Amur tiger, native to Russia, Northern China, and Mongolia and once hunted to just 40 animals in the 1940s, was the first tiger in the world to be given full protection. Nowadays, the hunting of tigers has generally become quite rare, however, the thing that helped the Amur tiger recover so rapidly was the restriction of hunting other animals. These included boars and deer that were the natural prey of the tiger. The continued protection of their environment and ban on hunting has allowed their numbers to recover to over 500 today.

GLOSSARY

genes (n) a pattern of chemicals within a cell that carries information about the qualities passed to a living thing from its parents

5 The food chain is intrinsically linked to the ecosystem of an area. If a key part of that ecosystem is damaged, then it can affect many other species. An example of one such animal is the mountain gorilla, which without the conservation efforts of some individuals and charities would possibly already be extinct. These organizations have worked with local communities and governments to protect the habitat of these gorillas. While there are only in the region of 700 alive today, and they are listed as critically endangered, if efforts had not been made, there could quite easily have been none left today. Another example of this is the recent pressures many bees have faced on their habitats. Without bees, crops would rarely be pollinated and major shortages of food would occur. People depend on the ecosystem to ensure their supply of food and water, and ecosystems being disrupted can have serious consequences.

6 Our actions may also have other consequences that we do not always realize. Take what many consider to be the first environmental success—protecting whales in the 1960s. At the time, this was little more than an exercise in protecting an endangered species. However, research shows that whales are vital to the oceans' carbon cycle because their iron-rich faeces feeds phytoplankton, organisms that absorb carbon dioxide. The more phytoplankton there are, the more carbon dioxide is absorbed. In the 20th century, some 300,000 blue whales were hunted from our oceans along with many hundreds of thousands of other whales. This not only endangered a species, but also caused a reduction in phytoplankton and possibly exacerbated the issue of climate change. Protecting whale populations could rebalance the ecosystem in our oceans and help reduce carbon levels in the atmosphere.

7 Another potential benefit comes from the economic boost provided from ecotourism, which has become big business for many local communities. Ecotourism seeks to reduce the damage traditionally caused by industries and to protect the local environment. Such was its success in Costa Rica that several national parks and reserves were created. Jobs such as tour guides are created as a result of ecotourism, while local businesses, from craftspeople to restaurateurs, can also benefit. In Costa Rica, it was found that this economic boost reduced the environmental damage caused by local activities as well.

8 Humans have had a detrimental effect on a range of wildlife throughout the world. No one solution will solve all of these challenges, but reacting to the local situation can assist in re-establishing animals once on the edge of extinction.

D Close reading

1 Read these sentences from *More than just survival*. In each sentence, circle the synonym of the underlined word or phrase.

1 In fact, a number of animals that were <u>close to dying out</u>, have actually been brought back from the edge of extinction.

2 There are a number of different <u>factors</u> that lead to the extinction or near extinction of an animal. One reason, especially in the past, was the over-hunting of an animal.

3 Twice hunted to near extinction, <u>the gray whale</u> was given protected status nearly 80 years ago, and hunting was limited to fewer than 200 annually. In the 1940s, the population had been hunted to fewer than 2,000.

2 Read paragraph 3 and identify the synonyms of these words.

1 challenges _____

2 low numbers _____

3 variety _____

3 Read *More than just survival* again and complete the sentences using no more than two words.

1 One way to conserve a species is to stop hunting of the rest of the _____.

2 The Amur tiger was the first tiger to get _____.

3 The mountain gorilla is _____ but could have been extinct if it hadn't been protected.

4 Humans rely on local environments for access to _____ and _____.

5 During the _____, huge numbers of whales were hunted.

6 Giving whales a protected status may lower _____ and reduce global warming.

E Critical thinking

Work in a group. Discuss the questions.

1 What do you think has had the biggest impact on the survival of animals?
The biggest threat is probably …

2 What is the best way to ensure the survival of a species?
The most effective way is probably …

Vocabulary development

Describing graphs

We use a range of vocabulary to describe points on a graph or to describe the approximate amount of something.

1 Match the words in bold with the correct definitions.

1	**comparison** (n)	a	slowly and gradually continuing to change, move, or happen
2	**growing** (adj)		
3	**in the region of** (phrase)	b	the process of considering how things are similar or different
4	**peak** (v)	c	used before a number for saying it is not exact and could be higher or lower
5	**slight** (adj)	d	to reach the highest level, before becoming lower
6	**steadily** (adv)	e	large in amount or degree
7	**substantial** (adj)	f	much higher than a number
8	**well over** (phrase)	g	small in size, amount, or degree
		h	used to describe things that are becoming greater in size or amount

2 Complete the sentences with words from Exercise 1. Change the form if necessary.

1 _____ a million people live in the city—perhaps close to one and a half million.

2 The population of bees _____ before starting to decline several years ago.

3 There are _____ numbers of gazelles in the region, with the population up around 25%.

4 While the growth was not dramatic, the figures rose _____ over the two decades.

5 There was a _____ fall in the number of rhinos, from over 20,000 to under 2,000.

6 There was a _____ fall in the fox population from 19,000 to 18,500.

7 No one knows exactly, but _____ 20,000 species are in danger of becoming extinct.

8 The graphs show a _____ of the different animal populations in 1980 and 2010.

3 Work with a partner. Use the words in Exercises 1 and 2 to describe changes in your country. Think about people, animals, languages, and changes to your hometown.

Academic words

1 Match the words in bold with the correct definitions.

1	**assist** (v)	a	to help someone or something
2	**discrimination** (n)	b	the way in which something is shared or spread over an area
3	**distribution** (n)	c	the fact that very different people or things exist within a group or place
4	**diversity** (n)		
5	**grant** (v)	d	to allow someone to have or do what they want
6	**inevitable** (adj)	e	unfair treatment of someone because of their religion, race, or other personal features
7	**minority** (n)	f	a small number of people or things that are part of a larger group, but different in some way from most of the group
8	**reverse** (v)		
		g	impossible to avoid or prevent
		h	to change the order or development of events, a process, or a situation to be the opposite of what it was

2 Complete the sentences with words from Exercise 1.

1 Even when a language is spoken by a _____ of people, it should be protected.

2 By taking action, it is possible to _____ the trend of a declining animal population and increase its numbers.

3 It is _____ that some species will become extinct and we should not worry about protecting them.

4 _____ of cultures makes a country more interesting.

5 Governments must _____ farmers in protecting the local environment.

6 The most effective way to protect a language is to _____ it a special status.

7 _____ of people for being different is usually a crime.

8 The _____ of animals can be improved. Some endangered animals could be reintroduced to areas they once lived.

3 Check (✓) the sentences you agree with in Exercise 2. Compare your ideas with a partner.

Critical thinking

Significant similarities and differences

When making a comparison or contrast, it is important to think why we are making a comparison. Things that are similar on a basic level can actually be quite different when analyzed. Take the classification of living things, for example. Biologists make judgements about the similarities and differences between different animals to decide whether they are the same species or a separate species. Factors such as breeding, anatomy, behavior, genetics, and evolutionary history can make two birds that look the same actually be defined as a different species.

1 **Read the analyses of the graphs below. Then compare the graphs in more detail with a partner.**

   1 A European language has fallen from just over 100,000 speakers to under 10,000 speakers in the last 50 years.

   2 A regional African language has fallen from just under 100,000 speakers to just over 10,000 speakers in the last 50 years.

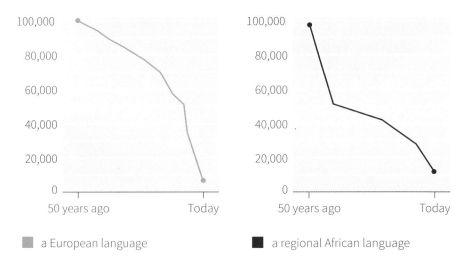

■ a European language   ■ a regional African language

2 **Think of the comparisons you made. How many focused on similarities and how many on differences.**

3 **Think about the reasons behind the differences. Explain the possible reasons for each difference.**

4 **Read the example question. Brainstorm other questions you could ask to focus on other differences.**

   How are the languages used today? For example, is one used in education, or politics?

Writing model

You are going to learn about using the present perfect progressive to write a description summarizing and comparing trends, and inferring reasons for changes. You are then going to use these to write a descriptive summary.

A Model

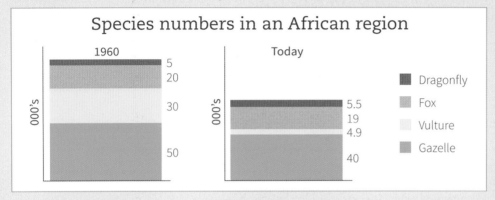

Species numbers in an African region

1 **Look at the graph and answer the questions.**

   1 What are the graphs comparing?

   2 Which changes are slight and which ones are substantial?

2 **Read the model and underline language describing changes.**

> The graph shows changes in the population of four animals in the Royal National Park between 1960 and today. The most substantial fall in population is in the number of vultures. Although the population remained stable until the year 1980, the numbers have been declining rapidly since then. Why they have dramatically decreased is uncertain—perhaps due to a fall in animal numbers in the region as a whole. The other species that have been declining are foxes and gazelles. The number of gazelles has been falling steadily since 1980, whereas the number of foxes has been declining slowly since the 2000s. While clearly not yet endangered, these falls may contribute to a decrease in diversity in the region unless the trend is reversed. Overall, most animal populations have been declining over recent years, possibly as a result of human activities. The only species that has been growing in number over the past 20 years is the dragonfly. This could be the product of conservation efforts that have assisted in reducing the destruction of the dragonfly's natural habitat.

B Analyze

1 **What do you think might be the main cause of the growth and decline for each of the animals below?**

> banning hunting   deforestation   hunting   increased farming
> introduction of conservation areas

   1 gorillas   2 rhinos   3 zebras   4 whales

2 **Compare your ideas with a partner.**

Grammar

Present perfect progressive

We use the present perfect progressive when an activity changes over a period of time or there is a connection to now.

has / have + been + -ing

*Although the population remained stable for much of the period from 1960 until the year 1980, the numbers **have been declining** rapidly since then.*

*The only species that **has been growing** in number over the past 20 years is the dragonfly.*

*Although the numbers **haven't been increasing** rapidly, there has been some growth.*

1 Complete the sentences using these verbs in the present perfect progressive.

decline   film   study   thrive   try   use

1 Television companies _____ the animals in their natural habitat to get a better understanding of their behavior.
2 Sadly, the cheetah population _____ for years.
3 Researchers _____ the genetics of the species for six months.
4 The zoo _____ to get the pandas to reproduce in captivity.
5 In recent years, the population _____ and the species is no longer considered to be endangered.
6 Recently, the animals have been hunted in large numbers again. As a result, the government _____ guards to protect the area.

2 For each situation, write a sentence using the words in parentheses.

1 The films crew started filming two days ago.
(the crew / film / for two days) _____
2 Bee numbers started to fall recently, and they are still falling today.
(bee numbers / fall / recently) _____
3 A new organization is working to change farming habits. Traveling for six months so far.
(the organization / travel / for six months) _____

3 Write sentences about these situations, using the present perfect progressive.

1 World population since 2000
2 Sea levels for the last 50 years
3 Renewable energy use since 2010

Writing skill

When interpreting data in a graph, it may be possible to infer why this change has happened. It is important to hedge these inferences carefully as you do not know for sure what the reasons are for change. Compare the additional information added here to make the second one more cautious:

The rise in elephant numbers was due to a ban on hunting.

The rise in elephant numbers may have been as a result of the ban on hunting, although there is no evidence for this in the data.

These phrases are typically placed in between the result and the possible cause.

1 Underline the phrases used to hedge the inferences.

1 The rise in elephant numbers may have been as a result of the ban on hunting, although there is no evidence for this in the data.

2 The fall in gazelle numbers is perhaps due to competing for land with farmers.

3 The growth in a number of animal populations could be the product of government policy.

4 The decline in gorilla numbers may have been due to the increased levels of deforestation.

5 The growing number of cod in certain regions could be attributed to the limits placed on the number of fish that can be caught.

6 The change in bird numbers could be a consequence of a loss of habitat.

2 Identify the reason for change in each of these sentences.

1 The tiger population fell due to hunting.

2 Tuna numbers have been falling because of overfishing.

3 Bison numbers grew as a result of a hunting ban.

4 Wolf numbers have been growing recently because a national park was created two years ago.

5 Otter numbers leveled off because of changes in government rules.

6 Hippo numbers are rising as a consequence of being given protected status.

3 Rewrite each sentence in Exercise 2 using a hedging expression. You may need to change the first verb phrase to a noun phrase.

Tuna numbers have fallen …

The fall in tuna numbers …

Writing task

You are going to write a descriptive summary in response to the following:
"This graph compares trends in animal populations. Write a summary describing the trends and give reasons for the changes."

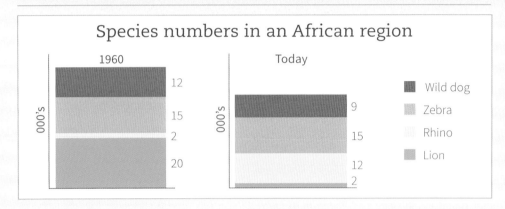

Brainstorm

Look at the graphs and make a note of the key differences.

Plan

Answer the following questions as you plan your description.

1 Which changes are slight or substantial?
2 What might be some reasons for these changes?

Write

Use your plan to help you write your summary. Remember to use the present perfect progressive as appropriate and infer reasons for the changes. Your text should be 150 words long.

Share

Exchange your summary with a partner. Use the checklist on page 189 to help you provide feedback to your partner.

Rewrite and edit

Consider your partner's comments and write your final draft. Think about:

- whether you described the main changes clearly
- whether you used the present perfect progressive appropriately
- whether you inferred reasons for the changes appropriately.

Review

Wordlist

MACMILLAN DICTIONARY

Vocabulary preview

breed (v) **	minority (adj)	threat (n) ***
commerce (n) **	nation (n) ***	thrive (v) *
die out (phr v)	official (adj) ***	urbanization (n)
disrupt (v) *	ruling (adj) **	widely (adv) ***
food chain (n)	shortage (n) **	
habitat (n) *	superior (adj) **	

Vocabulary development

comparison (n) ***	peak (v)	substantial (adj) ***
growing (adj) ***	slight (adj) ***	well over (phrase)
in the region of (phrase)	steadily (adv)	

Academic words

assist (v) ***	diversity (n) **	minority (n) ***
discrimination (n) **	grant (v) ***	reverse (v) **
distribution (n) **	inevitable (adj) **	

Academic words review

Complete the sentences with the words in the box.

assist   grant   inevitable   minority   virtually

1 Hunting has led to the _____ decline in the number of whales.

2 The government will _____ the funding for a new school.

3 Only a small _____ of people can understand my native language.

4 _____ everyone I know believes in protecting endangered species.

5 We need to _____ local communities so that they can develop tourism in the areas without causing damage to the environment.

Unit review

Reading 1	☐	I can find support for my opinion.
Reading 2	☐	I can use research questions.
Vocabulary	☐	I can use vocabulary for describing graphs.
Study skill	☐	I can avoid self-sabotage.
Grammar	☐	I can use the present perfect progressive.
Writing	☐	I can infer the meaning of data in graphs.

Discussion point

Discuss with a partner.

1 Rank the behaviors in the infographic from most concerning to least concerning.

I think … is the most / least concerning because …

2 Do you think each of these situations should be punished? How and why?

I don't think / think … should be punished because …

3 Whose responsibility is it to decide what is right and wrong?

I think it's the responsibility of … because …

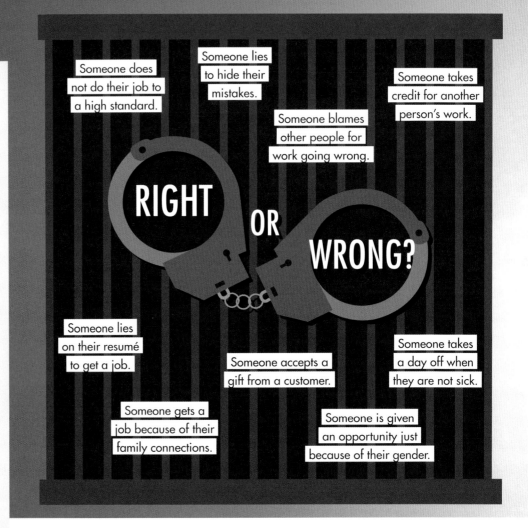

Someone does not do their job to a high standard.

Someone lies to hide their mistakes.

Someone takes credit for another person's work.

Someone blames other people for work going wrong.

RIGHT OR WRONG?

Someone lies on their resumé to get a job.

Someone accepts a gift from a customer.

Someone takes a day off when they are not sick.

Someone gets a job because of their family connections.

Someone is given an opportunity just because of their gender.

VIDEO

LIFESTYLE AND CONNECTIVITY

Before you watch

Match the words in bold with the correct definitions.

1 **burn-out** (n)
2 **hyper-connected** (adj)
3 **incompetence** (n)
4 **log off** (v)
5 **work-life balance** (n)

a a state of exhaustion
b close down a computer or smartphone
c not having the ability to do a job properly
d the amount of time spent working compared to the amount of time spent with family and leisure activities
e to be connected to technology all the time

UNIT AIMS

READING 1 Activating prior knowledge
READING 2 Summarizing a text
STUDY SKILL Argumentative writing

VOCABULARY Legal vocabulary
GRAMMAR Unreal conditionals in the past
WRITING Opposing views

Statue representing Themis, the Goddess of Justice.

While you watch

Read the sentences then watch the video. Write
T (True), or *F* (False).

1   The new French law will protect employees. ___

2   The law will protect them from spending too much
time at the office. ___

3   Office workers will receive 32 times more
information by 2020. ___

4   La Poste defines off-hours time as 7:30 a.m. until
8:00 p.m. on the weekends. ___

After you watch

Work with a partner. Discuss the questions.

1   Do you think such a law would work in your
country?
In my country … because …

2   What would the off-hours be in your country?
I think the off hours would be … because …

3   What other laws could you introduce to protect the
work-life balance?
I think we should introduce a law to … because …

It's legal, but is it ethical?

A Vocabulary preview

1 Complete the sentences with the words in the box. Change the form if necessary.

> a fine line   basis   break the law   ethics
> ideal   illegal   punishment   scandal

1 The difference between right and wrong should form the _____ of the law.

2 It's important for every company to have an _____ policy.

3 When someone _____, the _____ should reflect how serious the crime is.

4 In an _____ situation, no one would do anything _____. They would all follow the law.

5 A _____, such as avoiding tax, can affect a company's reputation and cause it to lose customers.

6 Sometimes it is _____ between right and wrong, so companies need to have clear rules for employees to follow.

2 Check (✓) the sentences you agree with in Exercise 1. Compare your answers with a partner.

B Before you read

Predicting

Read the heading. What do you think the text is going to cover?

C Global reading

Activating prior knowledge

> Often when you read a text you may not have been thinking about the topic beforehand. This can make it difficult to follow a text, especially if it is a topic you have not thought about for a while. Spending a moment thinking about what you already know on the topic can help your understanding.

1 Before you read *It's legal, but is it ethical?*, discuss these questions with a partner.

1 How do you define law?

2 What examples of unethical behavior can you think of?

3 How are ethics and the law different?

4 When might legal behavior be unethical?

5 When might unethical behavior affect what happens with the law?

2 Read the text. Does it cover any of the points you discussed?

It's legal, but is it ethical?

1 Society judges right and wrong in many different ways. There are legal, religious, and ethical interpretations that are commonly used in many societies to decide between what is good and bad. Ethics and law are closely connected and there is a fine line between the two. In many ways, laws are based on people's beliefs about what is right and wrong. However, clearly not all unethical behavior is illegal and not all legal behavior is ethical. To fully understand the difference, it is important to first define the two terms.

2 The law is a set of written rules and regulations, usually created by a legal institute or their representatives, such as judges and the government. It is thought to be accepted by the whole of society and something that is recognized and maintained by powers such as the police. Laws are created to keep the social order and to maintain peace and justice. They are there to protect the general public. The law clearly defines the things a person can or cannot do. If a law is broken, a punishment is enforced. This punishment varies depending on the significance of the crime. In general, most laws are created by society's ethical interpretations of right and wrong. However, ethics differs significantly from law.

3 As stated before, both ethics and law judge the difference between right and wrong. However, ethics has a very different position in society. Ultimately, ethics is an imagined ideal of what the perfect or best human being could be. The principles of ethics should guide people's decision-making about what is right and wrong, or at least fair. A key difference is that ethics is not written down or legally enforced. Each person will have their own view of right and wrong that will be formed by the people they know and the wider society they live in. Laws are regional, national, or even international. Ethics on the other hand is very much an individual concept.

4 Many legal things are often considered unethical. If someone told a serious lie but it was legal, many people would think of it as unethical. If someone broke a promise another person was strongly depending on, many would argue this was unethical. However, it is usually not illegal. Of course, a contract is essentially a promise that is protected by law, but promises are broken on a daily basis. People will only be judged by others and there will be no formal punishment associated with these. Therefore, how much a person is willing to lie is based solely on their own ethical principles. As everyone will have their own ethical code they live by, this is often the cause of many arguments and disagreements.

5 A more controversial area is when unethical behavior is thought to affect the wider society. There have been many scandals recently involving companies paying what is believed to be an unfair amount of tax. Tax is ultimately a way of redistributing money to make society fairer. It allows the provision of services such as schools and hospitals. There are laws to make sure people pay their taxes, and in many societies, these are punishable by a prison sentence. However, there is an important distinction between tax avoidance and tax evasion. Tax avoidance means trying to pay as little as possible without breaking the laws in a country. Tax evasion means breaking the laws by trying to pay as little as possible. The former is considered unethical by many people, but is in fact completely legal and no one could be arrested for this. There have been many examples recently, where corporate organizations earning billions of dollars have actually paid very little tax. In most cases, none have broken the law, yet many do not feel the companies are behaving ethically.

6 When unethical behavior affects many people, there is often a debate as to whether the law should be changed. By some estimates, in the region of 30% of large companies have paid little or no tax. Clearly, many people are not happy with this situation, including many governments. If they had paid all their taxes, more services could have been provided for the wider society. Companies argue that they are not breaking the law, but the wider society deems their behavior so unethical that the laws should change. This has caused various government ministries around the world to debate how companies are taxed so that tax avoidance becomes harder and companies have a legal obligation to pay more tax. While there are many proposed initiatives, it is often a slow process to make these legal.

7 Clearly, ethics alone is not enough to control the actions of individuals or organizations within a society. As ethics are based on individual values, they can be interpreted in wildly different ways. When unethical behavior is so extreme it affects the lives of many people, there is clearly a need to use this to change the law of a country.

D Close reading

Scanning

1   Read *It's legal, but is it ethical?* again. Are these statements *T* (True), *F* (False), or *NG* (Not Given)?

1   All unethical behavior is illegal. ___

2   Laws are usually spoken forms of rules. ___

3   Ethics are basically the same as a law. ___

4   Ethics vary from person to person. ___

5   Unethical people usually break the law. ___

6   Legal systems are the same everywhere in the world. ___

2   Complete the sentences with no more than three words from the text.

1   _____ and not keeping a promise are often not against the law, but people usually think they are unethical.

2   There is not usually a _____ for unethical behavior—only the opinions of others.

3   Taxes allow governments to run _____.

4   _____ is legally avoiding paying taxes.

5   _____ is illegal because companies are not following the tax laws of a country.

6   Governments want to make it _____ for companies to avoid tax.

E Critical thinking

Work in a group. Discuss the questions.

1   Should all unethical behavior be made illegal?
   Yes, it should because …
   No, it shouldn't because …

2   Is it OK to do unethical things as long as they are not illegal?
   No, because …
   Yes, because …

3   Who is responsible for judging unethical behavior?
   I think it's the responsibility of … because …

Study skills Argumentative writing

To argue a point of view effectively you need to do the following.

Don't be tempted to sit on the fence. You can sound cautious, and show that there are strong arguments on more than one side, but indicate which side you find most convincing.

Show that you have considered any possible arguments which might contradict your case.

Be able to demonstrate convincingly why your argument or position is the best.

© Stella Cottrell (2013)

1   Read the essay question. Discuss your opinion with a partner.

Tax avoidance is ethically wrong. Laws should be changed to make this harder for companies and people to do.

2   Which of these sentences follows the advice in the box?

1   Tax avoidance could be wrong and governments could think about changing the law.

2   Tax avoidance can result in people paying the wrong amount of tax and therefore the laws should be changed.

3   Tax avoidance is not illegal; however, it can result in unfair amounts of tax being paid, and consequently, laws should be changed.

3   Read the essay question and the two thesis statements. What is weak about the statements?

Unethical behavior should not be punished if it is legal. To what extent do you agree?

1   Unethical behavior is not good for society, but it is not illegal.

2   Unethical, but legal, behavior should be punished.

4   Write a thesis statement for the essay question in Exercise 3. State your opinion clearly and show that there are other arguments.

5   Compare your thesis statement with a partner and discuss the viewpoints you might discuss in your essay.

Right or wrong at work

A Vocabulary preview

1 Complete the questions with the words in the box. Change the form if necessary.

conduct   declare   extent   intention   occur   recruit   state   tactic

1 When companies _____ new employees, should they worry about the person's character?

2 Who is responsible for employee behavior and _____ at work?

3 To what _____ is a company responsible for its ethics?

4 If an employee's _____ are good, does it matter that their behavior is unethical?

5 What is the best _____ to get companies to behave ethically?

6 If a company clearly _____ its rules, should an employee always follow them?

7 Why does unethical behavior _____?

8 Should a company publicly _____ how much tax it pays?

2 Work with a partner. Discuss the questions in Exercise 1.

B Before you read

Preparing to read

What examples of unethical behavior in the workplace can you think of? How might companies try to improve employees' ethical behavior?

C Global reading

Reading for main ideas

Match the main ideas (A–H) to the paragraphs (1–8).

A Rules to control employee behavior   ____

B The ethics of presents   ____

C Unethical behavior in life and work   ____

D Covering up expenses   ____

E Cheating the tax system   ____

F Unethical behavior in work   ____

G Doing less work   ____

H Employing and keeping the best employees   ____

Right or wrong at work

1 Unethical behavior occurs in every part of life, but since most people spend a large part of their waking day at work, it is not surprising that a large proportion of this occurs while doing our jobs. This behavior can be very simple things such as taking a short cut to complete a task to taking credit for completing someone else's work. While it is unlikely that unethical behavior can ever be removed from the workplace, there are measures that can be put into place to encourage a more ethical working environment.

2 To a certain extent, unethical behavior is open to personal interpretation. For some, taking a short cut to complete a task might simply be perceived as an efficient way of working. However, to others, this may be seen as not completing the task to the best of your ability. Other behaviors, such as lying to hide mistakes, blaming someone else for your poor work, or taking a day off sick when you aren't actually ill, are much more likely to be thought of as unethical by a wider range of people. Even when something is done with good intentions, such as lying to hide a colleague's mistake, it can still be perceived as unethical by others. Of course, unethical behavior in the working environment can even occur before someone starts a job. Some surveys have found that more than 50% of the population lie on the resumé they use to apply for jobs.

3 While unethical behavior may frequently occur, there are a number of things companies can do to limit how often or serious these misdemeanors are. One common strategy a lot of companies use is to create a code of conduct. This document outlines how employees are expected to behave and is frequently issued when new employees start in a company. However, reinforcing this document each year or whenever unethical behavior occurs can remind people of the company's expectations. Also, making multiple people responsible for a process can encourage ethical behavior because people will act as a check on each other.

4 Of course, to a certain extent it is about hiring the right person in the first place. When recruiting, companies should not just hire on the ability to complete the given role. They should also consider the individual's values and how they are likely to behave. This will result not only in the task being completed well, but also in a manner that matches the company's values. Furthermore, praising people for the standard of work may also have a positive effect. Not only is praise a good motivator, but it will also lead to employee loyalty. A loyal employee is much more likely to be an ethical one.

CASE STUDY

5 The owner of Company A is away on vacation for a week. During her break, she has decided to trust her employees to simply do their work. On the first day, the employees arrive and leave each day at the expected start and finish time. As the week progresses, more and more employees arrive late and finish early. All of their tasks have been completed, but on average each person has worked ten hours fewer than expected. If all the employees had worked their full hours, more work could have been completed.

6 Employee B is in charge of a key account for the company. The company's ethics policy includes a clause that states that employees must declare all gifts over the value of $50. When the employee awards a new contract to a supplier, they are given flowers, chocolates, and perfume as a gift. Rather than declaring the gift, the employee decides to keep quiet. As time progresses, he receives more gifts from the supplier and regularly awards them more contracts than their competitors, even when the competing bids are lower. If he had offered the contract to another supplier, the company would have saved money.

7 Imagine Employee Y spent up to two hours of company time every day on social media. She also frequently used the company telephones to make private calls. Because she always achieved her targets every day, she thought this was perfectly acceptable.

Company policy bans social media use and private phone calls from work. From the supply closet, she also often took pens, pencils, and paper for her children to use at home. Since she sometimes worked from home, she believed it was fine to take these supplies home. There have been many witnesses to this, but no one has said anything to the bosses. If they had reported this, she could have lost her job.

8 Company X is very profitable, but the owner would like to minimize the amount of tax the company pays. Although most of their business happens around the world, they decide to register the company in a country with very low taxation rates, a procedure common for many big companies. They actually pay very little tax in the countries where they make most of their profit. As a result, the company has increased its profits by around 15%. The owners are now able to pay themselves multi-million dollar bonuses. After an inspection, it was decided that they are not evading tax illegally, but they are avoiding paying the maximum amount possible by using this policy. While this is not a crime, they do employ lawyers to defend their situation.

❶ Do you think each situation is unethical?

❷ Which situation is the most unethical? Why?

❸ What could be done in each situation to improve the ethical behavior?

GLOSSARY

clause (n) a part of a legal document or law that officially states that something must be done

D Close reading

> A summary often focuses in on a particular section of a text. It usually focuses in on a part particularly relevant to an essay question. When completing a summary of a text as a reading task, for example, on an exam, many of the blanks will focus on key nouns or noun phrases.

1 Complete the summary of paragraphs 1–4. Use no more than three words from the text for each answer.

Controlling ethical behavior at work

A big ¹_____ of unethical behavior happens at work. This is likely to always happen, but companies can use different ²_____ to limit this. A challenge is that this behavior depends on individual ³_____. Different people see things in different ways. There is a wide range of unethical behavior at work. Many people do not even tell the truth on their ⁴_____ they use to get a job. Companies can write a ⁵_____ to state how employees should behave. Companies also need to employ someone based on their ⁶_____. Lastly, ⁷_____ for good work can make them more loyal and less unethical.

2 Read the case study section again. Discuss the questions at the end of the section in groups.

E Critical thinking

Work in a group. Discuss the questions.

1 Which of the unethical behaviors in paragraph 2 do you think is the most serious? Why?

   I think … is the most serious because …

2 Do you think the advice for companies in paragraphs 3 and 4 would be effective? Why / why not?

   I think … would work because …

   I'm not sure … would work because …

Vocabulary development

Legal terms

1 Match the words in bold with the correct definitions.

1	**arrest** (v)	a	an illegal action or activity
2	**crime** (n)	b	someone whose job it is to make decisions in a court of law
3	**defend** (v)	c	a legal process of judging and punishing people
4	**judge** (n)	d	for the police to take someone to a police station because
5	**justice** (n)		they believe they have done something illegal
6	**lawyer** (n)	e	someone whose job it is to provide people with legal advice
7	**trial** (n)	f	the process of examining a case in a court of law and deciding
8	**witness** (n)		whether someone is guilty or innocent
		g	someone who sees a crime, accident, or other event happen
		h	to try to prove that someone is not guilty

2 Complete the sentences with words from Exercise 1.

1 A _____ often has to _____ people in court even when they think that person has committed a crime. However, all people, even guilty ones, have the right to be represented legally.

2 In some countries, a _____ is responsible for making the law as well as applying it.

3 A _____ to a crime can help prove whether someone is guilty or not.

4 When police _____ someone, they usually have a limited time to decide whether the person is guilty or not.

5 Most _____ that is committed is very minor, but it uses a lot of police time.

6 The _____ system is there to protect the rights of the general public.

7 During a _____, all of the evidence must be considered before deciding on the verdict.

3 Work with a partner. Discuss the questions.

1 Would you be happy to be a lawyer defending someone who committed a crime?

2 Should company ethics be based on laws?

3 What mistakes can be made when a judge decides whether a criminal is guilty or not?

Academic words

1   Match the words in bold with the correct definitions.

1   **code** (n)
2   **clause** (n)
3   **controversy** (n)
4   **corporate** (adj)
5   **initiative** (n)
6   **inspection** (n)
7   **institute** (n)
8   **ministry** (n)

a   a disagreement that a lot of people have strong feelings about

b   an organization that does a particular type of research or educational work

c   a set of rules about how something should be done or how people should behave

d   a government department responsible for one particular area, e.g., education

e   a part of a legal document or law that officially states that something must be done

f   an official process of checking that things are being done correctly

g   an important action that is intended to solve a problem

h   relating to large companies

2   Complete the sentences with words from Exercise 1.

1   The government has introduced an _____ to fight against tax avoidance.

2   The company's _____ of ethics does not allow employees to receive gifts.

3   The _____, reported widely in the media, affected the company's image badly.

4   The government _____ for tax and pensions is trying to develop rules that allow them to increase the amount of tax collected.

5   _____ organizations should be responsible for the behavior of their employees.

6   Employees have a _____ in their contract that means they can lose their jobs for unethical behavior.

7   The _____ of Business Ethics encourages high standards of business behavior based on ethics, but it has no control over how companies actually behave.

8   An _____ of the company's accounts led the police to believe that the organization had broken the law.

3   Work with a partner. Do you think companies should have a code of ethics and clauses in employees' contracts to try and control their behavior, or should they rely on individual ethics?

Critical thinking

Appeal to authority

One method some people use to convince others of their argument, is by referring them to a person or institution of authority. The argument is presented in such a way that the writer wants someone to believe an idea just because an "authority" claims it to be true or right. However, it is always important to question the position and validity of an authority.

> The decision was not legally binding and only represented just over half the population's view. However, the government believes it is the best way for the country to proceed. Since they are elected to power and have all of the social, economic, and political data of the country at hand, it is therefore the best decision.

1 **Read the student text and answer the questions.**

   1 Who is the expert in this text?

   2 What is weak about the students' claim?

2 **Read the statements made by people and institutes of authority. Which ones do you think could be weak?**

   1 A leading economic journalist believes it is the right decision.

   2 An economic institution has collected data showing the best and worst outcomes.

   3 A winner of the Nobel Prize for Economics thinks it is the wrong decision.

   4 A survey of 5,000 people shows that 75% of their personal financial situation has worsened in the last 12 months.

3 **Work with a partner. Discuss the questions.**

   1 Why do you think people use experts or authority figures to try to win arguments?

   2 Why is research generally held in higher regard than opinion?

   3 When might it help to refer to expert opinion?

Writing model

You are going to learn about using the unreal conditional in the past, and writing for-and-against essays. You are then going to use these to write an essay about speaking out against unethical behavior at work.

A Analyze

Read the brainstorm on the essay question. Organize the ideas into
F (For) and A (Against).

"Should workers speak out if their employers are unethical?"

It protects the wider society. ___

They could lose their job. ___

No crime is being committed. ___

It creates a fair situation for other companies. ___

An inspection might change the law. ___

The company will have lawyers to defend them. ___

B Model

1 Read the model and answer the questions.

   1 Circle the arguments from the brainstorm.

   2 Does the writer think employees should speak out or not?

   3 After the introduction, does the writer present the supporting arguments or the alternative position?

In recent times, there have been many controversies involving unethical behavior from companies. While their actions are not a crime, many feel that companies' ethics policies should make them behave fairly more. This essay will argue that if a company is behaving unethically, then an employee should speak out.

It could be argued that an employee does not always need to speak out. If a crime wasn't committed, then limited action could be taken by a judge. Even if a crime had happened, the employee would have needed significant proof to make a case. Large companies employ teams of lawyers to defend themselves, and at the very least, the worker can expect to lose their job.

However, many people would argue that the employee should take the initiative and try to force an inspection of the company. Corporate organizations are very influential in society and need to be challenged to protect the wider community. At a minimum, this would create a fair situation for companies to compete in, and may even result in laws being changed.

In conclusion, while there is some personal risk to the individual, and unethical behavior is not illegal, they should still speak out to protect the wider society. If no one had ever challenged a large corporation about its behavior, many important laws that protect everyone's interests wouldn't have been introduced.

2 How is it different to speak out about a company's behavior as opposed to a colleague's behavior? What are the different arguments for and against?

Grammar

Unreal conditionals in the past

Unreal conditionals in the past are used to talk about things happening in a different way than they really did. It is often used to point out mistakes or regrets.

If + past perfect + *would / could / should have* + past participle

If he **hadn't taken** the gifts, he **wouldn't have lost** his job.

If they **had worked** their full hours, the company **could have been** more productive.

1   Complete the sentences using the correct form of the verbs in parentheses. Use the symbols (– / +) to help you.

   1   If he _____ (break –) the law, he _____ (go –) to prison.

   2   If the company _____ (have +) a code of conduct, then employees _____ (know +) how to behave.

   3   If the ministry _____ (react +) quicker, then there _____ (be –) such a controversy.

   4   If all corporate organizations _____ (pay +) the full amount of tax, the government _____ (have +) a lot more money to spend.

   5   If the judge _____ (know +) about the additional evidence, the decision _____ (be +) different.

2   Correct the mistakes in these sentences.

   1   If you would have been more honest, you wouldn't have been in trouble.

   2   If I'd have known earlier, I wouldn't have done it.

   3   If I hadn't lied on my resumé, I would gotten the job.

   4   The company would have been in trouble if I report it.

   5   What would of happened if you had spoken out?

3   Read the following situations. Write sentences in the unreal conditional in the past to express how things might have been different.

   1   Someone didn't finish their work because they spent so much time on social media.

     If they hadn't spent so much time on social media, they would have finished their work.

   2   Someone made lots of mistakes in a report and the company made the wrong decision.

   3   Someone left confidential documents on a train and they were published in a newspaper.

Writing skill

When writing a for-and-against essay, it is important that your thesis statement clearly states your opinion.

In the main body, it is logical to present the opposing view first. For example, in an essay where the writer is in agreement with the statement in the question, the structure would be:

Introduction — for
Paragraph 2 — opposing views
Paragraph 3 — reasons for
Conclusion — summary of both arguments and a paraphrase of the thesis

1 Which of these thesis statements clearly show the writer's position?

   1 There are reasons for and against employees speaking out against unethical colleagues.

   2 People should speak out against unethical colleagues because their behavior could affect the company's performance.

   3 People shouldn't speak out against unethical colleagues because it may have a negative effect on their own career.

2 Put the phrases into the correct column in the table.

   Another viewpoint is   It can be argued that   It is my belief that
   One perspective is   Others have argued that   This essay will argue that

Stating the first viewpoint	Stating an alternative view	Giving the author's view

3 Read the thesis. Match the points to paragraph 2 or 3.

   This essay will argue that unethical colleagues should be reported because they often do not perform to the same standard as others.

   - blame others for their mistakes ___
   - an unethical attitude does not mean a low standard ___
   - do not complete work to the best of their ability ___
   - could badly affect the atmosphere ___
   - it is the company's responsibility not the employees ___
   - do not start and finish at the correct time ___

Writing task

You are going to write a for-and-against essay in response to the following:
"Should employees speak out if their colleagues are unethical?"

Brainstorm

Complete the brainstorm with your ideas.

For	Against

Plan

1 Are you for or against employees speaking out in this situation?

2 What examples could you use to support your points?

3 What might have happened if someone had / hadn't spoken out against an unethical colleague?

Write

Use your brainstorm to help you write your essay. Remember to use the unreal conditional in the past as appropriate and to structure your essay clearly. Your text should be 250 words long.

Share

Exchange your essay with a partner. Use the checklist on page 189 to help you provide feedback to your partner.

Rewrite and edit

Consider your partner's comments and write your final draft. Think about:

• whether you structured your essay clearly

• whether you used the unreal conditional in the past appropriately.

Review

Wordlist

MACMILLAN **DICTIONARY**

Vocabulary preview

a fine line (phrase)	extent (n) ***	recruit (v) **
basis (n) ***	ideal (adj) ***	scandal (n) **
break the law (phrase)	illegal (adj) **	state (n) ***
conduct (n) **	intention (n) ***	tactic (n) **
declare (v) ***	occur (v) ***	
ethics (n)	punishment (n) **	

Vocabulary development

arrest (v) **	judge (n) ***	trial (n) ***
crime (n) ***	justice (n) ***	witness (n) **
defend (v) ***	lawyer (n) ***	

Academic words

clause (n) *	corporate (adj) ***	institute (n) ***
code (n) ***	initiative (n) ***	ministry (n) ***
controversy (n) **	inspection (n) **	

Academic words review

Complete the sentences with the words in the box.

controversy	corporate	initiative	reverse	ultimately

1 The council is developing an _____ to tackle anti-social behaviour.
2 _____, it is up to the individual to decide what is right and wrong.
3 The judge refused to _____ her decision.
4 After the media found out about the company's actions, the _____ grew larger and larger.
5 People argue that ethics should be at the center of _____ law.

Unit review

Reading 1		I can activate prior knowledge.
Reading 2		I can summarize a text.
Vocabulary		I can use legal terms.
Study skill		I can argue a point of view effectively in writing.
Grammar		I can use the unreal conditional in the past.
Writing		I can write opposing views.

9 SOUND

SOUNDS IN OUR WORLD

Discussion point

Discuss with a partner.

1 What is different about the sounds animals make and the sounds people make?

   Humans are able to … but animals can't …

2 Is it important to understand more about animal communication?

   Yes, it is … because …

   No, it isn't … because …

3 Which invention do you think was the most significant in the infographic?

   I think … was the most important because …

The first ever recording was on a phonautograph.
Sound waves drew lines on paper or glass.

The first radio broadcast.

1900

1875
Alexander Graham Bell transmitted sounds by radio for the first time.

1927
The first movie with sound, *The Jazz Singer*, was released.

The first TV station was launched.

1928

1973
The first cell-phone call was made.

VIDEO

WHALES AND NOISE POLLUTION

Before you watch

Match the words in bold with the correct definitions.

1 **drill** (v)   a find the way (often at sea)

2 **interfere** (v)   b make a hole in something

3 **monitor** (v)   c prevent or obstruct something

4 **navigate** (v)   d watch and listen

UNIT
AIMS

READING 1 Using graphic organizers
READING 2 Note taking
STUDY SKILL What gets good marks?

VOCABULARY Science verbs
GRAMMAR Relative clauses
WRITING Explanations: Varying sentence length

The UK's biggest collection of vintage radios.

While you watch

Read these questions then watch and choose the correct answer.

1 Why did researchers place microphones on the seabed?

   a to monitor the sounds of whales

   b to monitor noise pollution

2 Who is responsible for the noise pollution?

   a man   b whales

3 What is the purpose of the network?

   a to warn whales about noise

   b to warn people when whales are approaching

After you watch

Work with a partner. Discuss the questions.

1 Have you ever seen dolphins or whales?

   Yes, I have. It was …

   No, I haven't …

2 Share what you know about whales.

   I know that …

3 Which do you think is more important, protecting whales or protecting jobs? Explain your choice.

   I think … is more important because …

Seeing without your eyes

A Vocabulary preview

1 Complete the text using the words in the box. Change the form if necessary.

> absorb   advance   air pressure   determine
> echo   reflect   sound wave   vibration

Six hundred years BCE, the Greek scientist Pythagoras proposed the principle that sound is caused by [1] _____ in the air. Essentially, these are moving and changing the [2] _____ around the sound. Not long after this, the process of sound traveling through the air to the ear drum was discovered. By the 19th century, our understanding had [3] _____ significantly. Research was now focusing heavily on the idea of [4] _____. This showed the frequency at which different sounds traveled. The number of waves per second [5] _____ the frequency. Researchers also started to understand the importance of the environment on the sound created. Some materials would [6] _____ the sound whereas others would [7] _____ the sound and rebound it back to the source, creating a strong [8] _____.

2 How do you think an echo is produced? Use the words in Exercise 1 to describe this process.

B Before you read

Activating prior knowledge

How do you think animals such as bats can see in the dark? Discuss your ideas with a partner.

C Global reading

Reading for main ideas

Read *Seeing without your eyes*. Match the headings (A–F) to the paragraphs (1–6).

A   The discovery of echolocation   ____
B   Our limited knowledge   ____
C   Unusual phenomenon in nature   ____
D   Echolocation and dolphins   ____
E   Using the environment and different sounds   ____
F   How echoes are produced   ____

Seeing without your eyes

1

The animal kingdom is full of surprising facts. From tarantulas, which are a species of spider, living for two years without eating food to ants that never sleep. One of the most fascinating parts of the animal kingdom is the way different species see. Snakes use their tongue to see and smell. Cats and dogs have amazing night vision. Perhaps two of the most remarkable creatures are bats and dolphins. Both exist in an environment that is difficult to see in and as a result, they have evolved to use different senses to see, travel, and hunt using echolocation.

2

An echo is produced in a very simple way. Air passes through the vocal chords to trigger a vibration. This vibration is a sound wave, which is essentially a fluctuation in the air pressure. These sound waves travel very quickly and in the right location, for example in a cave or a canyon, you will easily observe an echo of your own voice. The echo is the sound waves reflecting back in the direction of the speaker. With the right air conditions, the speed of the airwave does not change, and in principle, you could use the echo to figure out the distance to the back of the cave. In a very simplistic manner, this is how echolocation works.

3

The phenomenon of echolocation was first proposed as a principle over 100 years ago, and has been proven to exist for around 70 years. Although many bats can actually see as well as humans, this is not sufficient when your environment requires you to hunt small insects in total darkness. Bats make sounds that echo back to them to give them a better understanding of where things are in their environment. They use this method to hunt for food by processing the returning sounds. In other words, bats internally calculate the location of their prey based on the echo. How long it takes the sound to return, and the intensity at which the sound returns, helps the bat detect the location of an object or its prey. A bat is even able to identify the size of the animal it is hunting by the returning sound waves. Small prey will return a less intense sound and larger prey will return a stronger sound. Bats even use this technique to interpret the direction their prey is moving in.

4

Bats produce both constant frequency sounds, which travel long distances, and varying frequency sounds. It is these varying frequencies that give bats more detailed information about their environment. They also produce these sounds at an incredibly high level, much higher in fact than your average stereo speaker. However, the frequency of this sound is too high for humans to hear. Bats' brains and ears are adapted to hear this sound back at a much lower volume, but to also process the information at an incredible speed. In much the same way we gather information with our eyes and ears, bats process all of this information subconsciously and rapidly.

5

One of the other main species of animal to use echolocation is a dolphin. Similarly to a bat, dolphins exist in an environment that is difficult to see in using just their eyes. Dolphins use echolocation by producing the clicking sound for which they are famous. The principle for how the sound is made, how it travels, and how the dolphins use the sounds is basically the same as bats, but they benefit from the fact that sound waves travel five times faster through water than air. However, the part of the body used by dolphins to process the sound is different. Dolphins receive the sounds back to the fat around their jaw and their large forehead before their brains then process this information. Although it has been known that dolphins echolocate for over 60 years, much is still unknown about exactly what dolphins can see in their environment.

6

According to scientists, dolphins have been in existence for around 25 million years and bats for more than 50 million years. However, we have only known about their abilities for a relatively short period of time. Consequently, while we know the basic principles of their abilities, scientists are working to gain further insights into these skills.

> **GLOSSARY**
>
> **prey (n)** an animal hunted by other animals

D Close reading

Creating a text map

There are many different ways to organize your notes while you are reading. One way is to show the connections between different points by using a text map. This method shows the connection between different ideas in the text.

1 Read *Seeing without your eyes* and complete the text map.

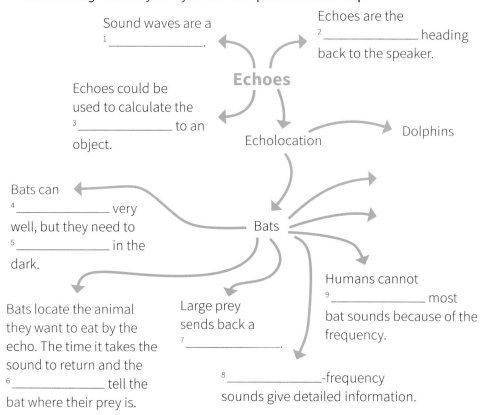

Sound waves are a
1_____.

Echoes are the
2_____ heading back to the speaker.

Echoes

Echoes could be used to calculate the
3_____ to an object.

Echolocation

Dolphins

Bats can
4_____ very well, but they need to
5_____ in the dark.

Bats

Bats locate the animal they want to eat by the echo. The time it takes the sound to return and the
6_____ tell the bat where their prey is.

Large prey sends back a
7_____.

Humans cannot
9_____ most bat sounds because of the frequency.

8_____-frequency sounds give detailed information.

2 Read the part about dolphins in *Seeing without your eyes* and create your own text map for this section.

E Critical thinking

Work in a group. Discuss the questions.

1 What modern technologies would we not be able to use without an understanding of echolocation and sound waves?

2 Sonar technology works in a similar way to echolocation. Look at the animals. Think of an ability of each that people might want to use in a product.

spider (**web**)   shark (**skin**)   gecko (**feet**)

People might want to copy the skin of a shark because of the speed it moves through water.

Study skills   What gets good marks?

To get good marks, you do not necessarily have to work longer hours. You do need to:

- Identify the task or problem
- Discover the underlying issues
- Find out exactly what is expected of you

If your college provides marking criteria, check these before you start your assignment, and use them as you work on it.

Go through drafts of your assignments, checking them against marking criteria.

© Stella Cottrell (2013)

1   Work with a partner. Think about an assessment you have both done and brainstorm the things the teacher was marking.

Evaluation of evidence

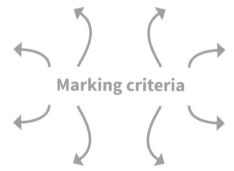

Marking criteria

2   Read the last piece of writing you did in this class and the criteria you thought of in Exercise 1. Underline parts of your work that demonstrate a good ability in these criteria.

3   Read the final task you will need to complete on page 168. Discuss with a partner what you think the criteria for the task will be, and then plan how you can approach the task.

A wireless world

A Vocabulary preview

Complete the sentences with the words in the box.

accelerate   broadcast   incredibly   interference
launch   network   satellite   unreliable

1 Two and a half million TV sets were sold in the U.K. to watch the
   _____ of Queen Elizabeth becoming queen.
2 The _____ of *Sputnik 1* started a revolution in telecommunications.
3 Old radio frequencies suffered from a lot of _____ before FM radio.
4 The development of technology can _____ very rapidly during
   certain periods.
5 _____ were first used for TV in the 1960s.
6 _____, many things originally mentioned in science-fiction books
   have actually become reality.
7 The "Internet of Things" is a concept where everything electronic will
   eventually be connected to a _____.
8 _____ wireless Internet connections make it difficult for many to
   access streaming services like Netflix or Amazon Prime.

B Before you read

Preparing to read

1 **Work with a partner. Which of the following inventions do you think have
   changed the world the most? Rank them from most to least important.**

   telephone   television   satellites   Wi-Fi

2 **How many things can you think of that work using wireless technology?**

C Global reading

Reading for main ideas

Match the headings (A–F) to paragraphs (1–6).

A The development of wireless technology   ____

B Satellite communications   ____

C The future of wireless   ____

D Communication before wireless technology   ____

E A computer in your hand   ____

F Intercepting and hiding communication   ____

A wireless world

1 The legend of Pheidippides describes a Greek solider and runner who is said to have run from Marathon to Athens to report the news of a military victory against the Persians at the Battle of Marathon. Communication over a great distance has proven to be a challenge for people for centuries. Empires extended over huge land masses, so passing a message from one location to another was an onerous task that could take months. For centuries, the main way to take a message from one location to another was by person on horseback, until the telegraph and Morse code were developed in the early to mid-1800s. Even then, communication was limited to the length of the wire it traveled through. The theory of wireless communication was being developed at a similar time, but it would be much later before this became reality. What happened would go on to transform many aspects of the modern world.

2 The field of wireless and telecommunications has a long history. James Clerk Maxwell first proposed the theoretical and mathematical form of wireless communication in 1864, but it wasn't until 1888 that Heinrich Rudolf Hertz conclusively proved that wireless communication could work. At this time, scientists were experimenting all around the world with technology that would lead to the development of both the radio and the telephone. Alexander Graham Bell and Guglielmo Marconi are respectively credited with the invention of the telephone and the radio. While both were the first to patent the technology, there were many other scientists and inventors developing similar technology and all building on the work of others in the field.

3 Wireless communication was initially very unreliable, but some devastating world events helped push the technology forward at a rapid speed. More stable and reliable technology, such as wideband frequency modulation (FM) radio, patented in 1914, significantly reduced noise and interference, and radio communications became the common way for people to communicate remotely. During the next 30 years, the globe would go through two devastating World Wars and radio communication would play a key role in many battles. Enemies quickly learned how to intercept each other's messages, and systems needed to be developed to protect these. The field of cryptology, which is the hiding of a message in a code, became vital in hiding knowledge and plans from the enemy. One of the most famous was the Enigma code machine used by Germany in the Second World War. It was this development that shortened the length of the war considerably.

4 One of the great leaps forward in wireless communication and technology came through the development of satellite technology. The idea was actually first proposed by the scientist and novelist Arthur C. Clarke in the British magazine *Wireless World*. The first artificial satellite put into orbit was *Sputnik 1*. The satellite was primarily launched for the purposes of rocket development and space exploration, but at the same time it had an on-board radio transmitter installed. Over the coming decades, more than 2,000 communications satellites were launched into Earth's orbit. Increasingly, television channels became broadcast via satellite, phone calls could be made in remote areas with no ground network, and the early stages of the Global Positioning System (GPS) were developed. Today's GPS network involves up to 30 satellites and is used in technology from route-finding to earthquake research to outdoor treasure-hunting games.

5 Another area of wireless technology that has transformed modern life is the use of cell phones. The technology has been around for decades, and cell phones have been incredibly popular since the mid-90s. What pushed the field forward further was the launch of Apple's first iPhone in 2007 and the subsequent rise of the smartphone. These have risen in popularity so rapidly that most people would probably rather give up their television and PC than their smartphone. In part, this is due to their processing ability, which is better than any computer from just a few decades earlier. Their connectivity is also important. In developing countries, cell phones have been key to providing access to the banking system. This has been vital to growing small entrepreneurial businesses because it allows them to access and transfer money easily. Furthermore, Whatsapp allows free messaging that small businesses can access readily. Essentially, many small businesses can be set up and run wirelessly from a smartphone.

6 None of this would have been possible without the development and constant improvement of Wi-Fi access and technology around the world. The once slow, dial-up Internet connections are very much a thing of the past as Wi-Fi speeds become faster and connections become more reliable. One possible future development in this area is Li-Fi technology, which if it works as well as the inventors hope, could accelerate Internet connection by up to 100 times. Wi-Fi currently sends data through buildings to your laptop or PC. Li-Fi will use lights to communicate much like a superfast Morse code. Current laboratory tests of Li-Fi allow for dozens of movies to be downloaded every second. While still a long way from being practical in the real world, it seems wireless technological developments show no signs of slowing down.

7 To people who used and developed the original wireless technology, today's world perhaps seems like science fiction. If technology continues to develop at this pace, what will the reality of another 150 years bring?

D Close reading

> Making notes in an academic context is often done with another purpose in mind, for example, to prepare for a seminar, to write an essay, and to prepare for an exam. Notes need to highlight the main points, and importantly, make sense at a later date when you might not have access to the text. Notes can be organized in a number of ways: linear (from start to finish of a text), in a spider diagram on different themes, etc.

Making notes

1 Read the notes for paragraph 1. Underline the words in the paragraph the writer has used or paraphrased.

Distant communication previously a challenge

Messages could take months on horseback

Changed by telegraph and Morse code, but distance still limited

2 Read paragraphs 2–4 in *A wireless world* again and complete the notes. Use no more than two words in each blank.

James Clerk Maxwell [1] _____ wireless communication in 1864. In 1888, Hertz showed it could [2] _____. Bell and Marconi [3] _____ the radio and telephone, but other people were also inventing similar devices.

Wireless communication improved with [4] _____ radio. During wars, it became important to [5] _____ enemy messages and to [6] _____ your own messages. [7] _____ was first suggested by Arthur C. Clarke. The first satellite was [8] _____.

Now there are over [9] _____ satellites. [10] _____ involves a network of 30 satellites.

3 Read paragraphs 5–7. Underline key ideas and make notes on each paragraph. Try to write no more than seven short sentences in total.

4 Compare your notes with a partner. Have you included the same information?

E Critical thinking

Work in a group. Discuss the questions.

1 How would communication change if modern technology no longer worked?

2 Do you think sound and technology should be considered a pollutant? Why / why not?

Vocabulary development

Science verbs

1 Match the verbs in bold with the correct definitions.

1	**calculate** (v)	a	to say what you think is wrong or bad about something
2	**classify** (v)	b	to write something, especially when this involves thinking carefully about it
3	**compose** (v)		
4	**criticize** (v)	c	to suggest a plan, idea, or action
5	**observe** (v)	d	to make a movement or sound that has a special meaning to another person
6	**propose** (v)		
7	**signal** (v)	e	to put people or things into groups or categories according to shared qualities or characteristics
8	**underline** (v)		
		f	to make a judgment about what is likely to happen or likely to be true using the available information
		g	to notice someone doing something, or to notice something happening
		h	to emphasise something or show that it is important

2 Choose the correct word to complete the sentences.

1 Some animals use movement to **signal / underline** danger to other animals.

2 Biologists determine different species by **classifying / composing** different animals into groups.

3 The film crew spent three months **categorizing / observing** the behavior of snow leopards.

4 The theory lacks scientific evidence and has been widely **criticized / underlined**.

5 Bats use sounds to **calculate / signal** how far away an object is.

6 The results **underlined / composed** the importance of the development.

7 The study was **composed / proposed** of four different stages.

8 Pythagoras was one of the first people to **propose / criticize** theories of sound.

3 Work with a partner. Discuss the questions.

1 What can scientists identify through observing people and animals?

2 Many scientific ideas proposed have later been identified as inaccurate. Does it matter that scientists propose incorrect theories?

3 What scientific processes do you most remember learning about at school?

Academic words

1 Match the words in bold with the correct definitions.

1	**comprise** (v)	a	to consist of two or more things
2	**device** (n)	b	happening, existing, or done before a particular time
3	**dominate** (v)		
4	**insight** (n)	c	an event or situation that can be seen to happen or exist
5	**phenomenon** (n)		
6	**prior** (adj)	d	to control something or someone, often in a negative way, because you have more power or influence
7	**thereby** (adv)		
8	**trigger** (v)	e	to cause something to happen
		f	because of, or by means of, what has just been mentioned
		g	a machine or piece of equipment that does a particular thing
		h	a clear, deep understanding of something

2 Complete the sentences with words from Exercise 1. Change the form if necessary.

1 The sight of danger can _____ different responses in animals.

2 _____ to the development of mobile communication, working processes were very different.

3 While scientists have gained some _____ into animal behavior, much is still unknown.

4 The process _____ ten individual steps.

5 The _____ of wireless communication continues to transform modern life.

6 The smartphone is a _____ that has revolutionized modern life.

7 Human language is _____ different from animal communication because of the abilities described previously.

8 Technology companies now _____ lists of the most valuable companies in the world.

3 Work with a partner. Discuss the questions.

1 What technological devices or phenomenon have most affected modern lives?

2 How can companies use technology to gain insights into customers' lives?

3 Is it positive or negative that technology dominates modern life so much?

Critical thinking

Logical order

It is important that an argument should have a clear direction and that each point should lead logically from one to another. Ideas should not be in a random order or move from one point to another without a sense of logic.

> Technology improves the quality of life. The benefits we observe outweigh the negatives. However, it can trigger a breakdown in relationships. Technology dominates and enhances communication. Prior to modern communication methods, families spent more time together. Many people use wireless devices to enable faster communication at work. The growth of technology companies underlines the importance of such developments to society.

1 **Read the paragraph and answer the questions.**

   1 Is there a main point to the paragraph?

   2 Are the ideas in a logical order?

2 **Read the following advice. Use the advice to rewrite the paragraph. Add your own ideas and examples as you write.**

   • Organize ideas into related groups, e.g., positive and negative

   • Include reasons to support your point

   • Think about alternative reasons and why these are not as valid as your main point

3 **Work with a partner. Discuss the questions.**

   1 Why is it important to organize ideas in a connected way?

   2 How do reasons enhance your argument?

Writing model

You are going to learn about using relative clauses. You are then going to use these to write an essay explaining how technology has influenced communication.

A Analyze

1 Read the brainstorm. Do you think the essay will argue technology has had a positive or negative effect on communication at work?

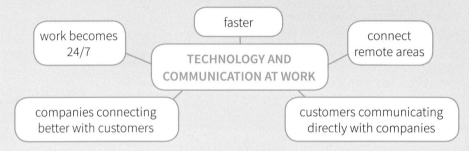

B Model

Read the model and answer the questions.

"How has technology affected the way people communicate at work? Has this been a positive or negative development?"

Technology has triggered many changes in the way people live and work. From the way we communicate to how we shop, travel, and complete everyday tasks, we can observe dramatic developments. While we can identify some negatives in these changes, this essay proposes that technology has transformed communication at work for the better.

Speed is the most significant change. Prior to the Internet and cell devices, the distribution of people across long distances significantly slowed down communication. While landlines enabled faster communication, it was the vast improvements in cell technology that signaled a revolution in working practices.

Alongside this, the World Wide Web changed communication at work that not only influenced how employees communicate with each other, but also how companies communicate with their customers. The Internet meant companies could identify possible customers online and communicate with them. Equally, consumers could engage publicly with companies and highlight any dissatisfaction with products or service.

In conclusion, the technological developments of the recent decades that have made communication more efficient and effective. Communication between customers and companies has also changed, meaning companies can more effectively market products and customers can hold companies accountable.

1 How is the question "Has this been a positive or negative development?" different from "What are the positives and negatives of this development?"?

2 How could you argue that technology has been a negative development?

Grammar

Defining and non-defining relative clauses

Defining relative clauses provide essential information that cannot be left out of the sentence. We do not use commas in defining relative clauses.

Li-Fi is a type of technology that uses light to communicate.

In defining relative clauses we can leave out the relative pronoun if it is the object of the clause.

Non-defining relative clauses provide additional information that is not essential to the meaning of the sentence. If we remove the non-defining clause, the sentence still makes sense. We use commas in non-defining relative clauses.

Bats produce both constant frequency sounds, which travel long distances, and varying frequency sounds.

1   Read the following sentences and decide if they contain defining or non-defining relative clauses.

   1   Scientists were experimenting all around the world with technology that would lead to the development of both the radio and the telephone.

   2   Whatsapp allows free messaging that small businesses can access readily.

   3   Hearing aids, which are designed to improve hearing, need to be adapted to each individual for the best possible results.

   4   Waves which travel through the Earth's layers after an earthquake are called seismic waves.

   5   The field of cryptology, which is the hiding of a message in a code, became vital in hiding your knowledge and plans from the enemy.

2   Underline any relative pronouns that can be left out in the following sentences.

   1   Some animals that hunt in the dark use echolocation to locate their prey.

   2   The lecture that I attended yesterday was about sonar technology.

   3   The smart TV that he bought last week has already broken.

   4   Human echolocation is a technique that some blind people use to help them navigate their environment.

   5   The developer is working on a new app that uses Li-Fi technology.

Writing skill

> Writers vary the length of their sentences for a number of different reasons.
> Often a short sentence is used to get the reader's attention. For example:
>
> *The animal kingdom is full of surprising facts.*
>
> These short sentences are then usually followed by a longer sentence that
> gives an explanation and more details. For example:
>
> *From tarantulas, which are a species of spider, living for two years without
> eating food to ants that never sleep.*

1   Match the short sentences (1–4) to their explanations (a–d).

1   Biomimicry is copying nature.

2   Sonar exhibits principles of echolocation.

3   Li-Fi may revolutionize wireless communication.

4   Twitter has shortened communication.

a   By transmitting a signal out, and receiving one in return, a ship is able
to calculate the distance to a fixed object or identify the bottom of the
seabed.

b   A tweet is comprised of just 140 characters, through which an individual
must convey their message.

c   It involves looking at naturally occurring phenomenon, and then using
these insights in the construction of manmade products or components.

d   It is comprised of a series of lights that detect each other and interpret
data thousands of times faster than is currently possible.

2   Write longer sentences to explain each of these sentences.

1   Social media affects every relationship.

_____

2   Technology changed communication between colleagues.

_____

3   The telephone changed communication forever.

_____

4   Wearable technology is changing communication further.

_____

3   Think about the key ideas you might want to include in your essay. Tell your
partner about these in one short sentence. Then explain the idea further.

Writing task

You are going to write an essay in response to the following:

"How has technology affected the types of relationships people have? Has this been a positive or negative development?"

Brainstorm

Complete the brainstorm.

TECHNOLOGY CHANGING COMMUNICATION

Plan

Answer the questions.

1   How have the changes affected the types of relationships people have?
2   Is the impact of technology on communication and relationships mainly positive or negative?

Write

Use your brainstorm and plan to help you write your essay. Remember to use relative clauses where appropriate and varying sentence length. Your text should be 250 words long.

Share

Exchange your essay with a partner. Use the checklist on page 189 to help you provide feedback to your partner.

Rewrite and edit

Consider your partner's comments and write your final draft. Think about:

- whether you answered the question clearly
- whether you used relative clauses appropriately
- whether you used varying sentence length.

Review

Wordlist

MACMILLAN DICTIONARY

Vocabulary preview

absorb (v) **	echo (n) *	satellite (n) **
accelerate (v) *	incredibly (adv) *	sound wave (n)
advance (v) **	interference (n) **	unreliable (adj) *
air pressure (n)	launch (v) ***	vibration (n) *
broadcast (v) **	network (n) ***	
determine (v) **	reflect (v) ***	

Vocabulary development

calculate (v) **	criticize (v) **	signal (v) **
classify (v) **	observe (v) ***	underline (v) **
compose (v) **	propose (v) **	

Academic words

comprise (v) **	insight (n) **	thereby (adv) **
device (n) ***	phenomenon (n) **	trigger (v) **
dominate (v) **	prior (adj) ***	

Academic words review

Complete the sentences with the words in the box.

diversity	dominate	exposure	prior	triggered

1   The Internet has begun to _____ our lives.
2   As far as possible, we want to increase people's _____ to the latest technologies.
3   _____ to television, radio was a popular source of entertainment.
4   We have seen smartphones _____ huge changes in the way we communicate.
5   The World Wide Web is a place which celebrates cultural _____.

Unit review

Reading 1	☐	I can use graphic organizers.
Reading 2	☐	I can make notes.
Vocabulary	☐	I can use science vocabulary.
Study skill	☐	I can recognize what gets good marks.
Grammar	☐	I can use relative clauses.
Writing	☐	I can vary sentence length in explanations.

10 TOMORROW

GLOBAL PREDICTIONS FOR 2050

The world's population will reach just under **10 BILLION** people.

1 IN 6 PEOPLE WILL BE **OVER 65** YEARS OLD.

Many people will live to **120 YEARS OLD.**

Diseases such as **MALARIA** will be easily **VACCINATED** against.

Computers will be ▶▶▶▶▶▶▶▶▶▶ **THOUSANDS OF TIMES FASTER.**

SOLAR POWER will be the world's main source of energy.

FOOD SHORTAGES around the world could **LEAD TO WAR.**

Cars and buildings will incorporate **MORE TECHNOLOGY** and **OPERATE INTELLIGENTLY.**

 Newspapers will **NO LONGER EXIST.**

Discussion point

Discuss with a partner.

1 Which prediction do you find the most interesting / exciting / worrying?

   The most ... is ... because ...

2 Many predictions are often inaccurate. Why do you think it's so hard to predict the future?

   It's hard to predict the future because ...

3 Make three other predictions about 2050. Discuss your predictions in groups.

   I think ...

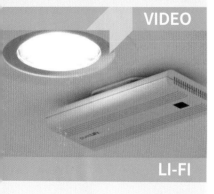

VIDEO

LI-FI

Before you watch

Match the words in bold with the correct definitions.

1 **bulb** (n)
2 **infrared** (adj)
3 **receiver** (n)
4 **signal** (n)
5 **transmitter** (n)

a a device that can receive electronic messages
b a device that sends messages
c a type of light that cannot be seen by the human eye
d an electrical glass object used to create light
e an electronic message

UNIT
AIMS

READING 1 Identifying conclusions and reasons
READING 2 Predictions in texts
STUDY SKILL Overcoming writer's block

VOCABULARY Science nouns
GRAMMAR Future perfect simple
WRITING Persuasive arguments

Solar power project on a roof, China.

While you watch

Watch the video and then choose the correct answer.

1   Li-Fi can be used **anywhere there is a light source / only in homes and driverless cars**.

2   Li-Fi uses **light to transmit Internet connectivity / rapid changes in the Internet signal**.

3   The company expects the price of the devices to **increase / decrease**.

4   The main problem with Li-Fi is that **it's very expensive / light only travels in straight lines**.

After you watch

Work with a partner. Discuss the questions.

1   Do you think you will be using Li-Fi soon?

   I think so / I don't think so because …

2   How do you think these things will change over the next 10 to 20 years?

   energy production   food   medicine   travel

3   If you could invent something new, what would it be?

   I would like to invent … because …

Products of the future

A Vocabulary preview

Complete the sentences with the words in the box.

devastating efficiency filter obsolete
particle properties revolutionary tackle

1 Many new products are developed to try to _____ a problem that exists.

2 A _____ event such as a tsunami can endanger thousands of lives.

3 It's a _____ material that could dramatically change hundreds of different areas.

4 Many technological developments eventually become _____ as new products emerge.

5 Many people _____ tap water to make it taste better.

6 A _____ is a tiny element that is part of an atom, such as an electron, proton, or neutron.

7 Scientists and product developers often look at the _____ of new materials and how they can be used in different ways.

8 Much research is done to improve the _____ of things that already exist.

B Before you read

Preparing to read

Work with a partner. Discuss the questions.

1 Which do you think are the most revolutionary products ever designed?

2 Why do some products become obsolete?

3 Why are so many developments focused on efficiency?

C Global reading

Reading for the main idea

Read *Products of the future*. Complete the text with the correct headings.

Environmental impact

Medical miracle

The most important discovery of the future?

The next Industrial Revolution

Water shortages

Revolutionizing IT and mobile communications

Products of the future

1

Every so often, a material or a product emerges that transforms the world. From the engine, to the discovery of electricity, to the development of the Internet: Each has transformed societies and changed lives. Many people now perceive the next big game changer as graphene, which is derived from graphite. This material exhibits many unique qualities. It can withstand strong force because it is around 200 times stronger than steel. It conducts electricity more efficiently than copper, and is more flexible than rubber. In the ten years since being isolated and studied, more than 7,000 patents for its use have been registered. So, what are some of the potential uses of this revolutionary product and how likely are they to happen?

2

After their investigations, researchers at Georgia Tech University believe it will be possible to make an ultra-thin antenna for cell phones that would allow a terabit of data to transfer in just one second. In other words, around 100 high-definition movies in just a few minutes. While this technology works in theory, the manufacturing process is still some way from being developed. Furthermore, all of the other components need to be made to work with the new antenna. Not only could data speeds be much more rapid, but the speed to charge a battery could increase at an incredible rate. Researchers at UCLA have developed a method to produce graphene batteries that charge in seconds. Measurements show that an iPhone could be fully charged in just five seconds and most laptops in just 30 seconds. Not only are they fast, they are also better for the environment because they are biodegradable. Unlike speeding up data transfer, these batteries may not be too far from production as researchers at Rice University have developed a process to make these on an industrial scale.

3

Arguably, the world doesn't need another product that will make millions of others obsolete. The amount of waste produced by society is already at dangerously high levels. However, graphene might not have such a devastating effect on the environment as some of its predecessors. As mentioned above, not only is the decay rate of these batteries faster, but it could also help tackle environmental disasters. Researchers at Rice University and Lomonosov Moscow State University have found evidence that graphene oxide has the ability to remove radioactive material from water incredibly quickly, thus potentially enabling the clean-up of nuclear disasters such as Fukushima. Research also shows that it could make nuclear energy production up to ten times more efficient and therefore more sustainable.

4

With predictions for the world's population to grow by up to another 30% by 2050, there is great concern for the supply of food and fresh water. However, researchers at the University of Manchester believe it may soon be possible to use filters made from graphene to remove salt from seawater, providing an endless supply of fresh drinking water. The process is also incredibly fast—similar to that of filtering coffee. Should this technology progress as researchers believe it will, the world will no longer be threatened by the potential shortage of water.

5

Graphene is also being tested for its potential use in the medical world and early biomedical research has had excellent results. Again, it is its unique structure and properties that make it such an exciting product. Graphene has been shown to potentially both detect and treat many forms of cancer. Chinese scientists have shown that it can be used to create a sensor that can detect even a single cell. It has also been shown to be able to target and reduce the size of tumors. It even helps to deliver large amounts of cancer drugs to specific parts of the body. While this research is still in its infancy, it shows great promise and has the potential to revolutionize many medical fields.

6

Currently, graphene is used in very few products or processes. However, research shows that its potential impact is arguably one of the most exciting in recent times. Many new discoveries eventually lead to greater environmental damage, but graphene has the potential to significantly reduce our negative impact on the world. Rarely has such a flexible and useful material been discovered. From simply making your tennis racquet better, to saving the lives of millions, graphene could well be the material that brings about the next great Industrial Revolution.

GLOSSARY

antenna (n) a long, thin piece of metal used to receive radio or television signals

biodegradable (adj) substances or chemicals that can be broken down by bacteria without harming the environment

terabit (n) a unit of computer information equal to 1,000 gigabytes

Understanding conclusions

D Close reading

Texts not only have conclusions at the end, but many draw small conclusions throughout. This is especially true when a text covers numerous different topics. Identifying these conclusions and reasons can help you to understand the author's point of view better.

1 Read *Products of the future* again and match the development with the conclusion.

1	Data transfer speeds	a	Technology needs to progress before this will work
2	Battery charging	b	Unlikely yet because many other products need to be developed
3	Water filtering	c	This has only just started but could have a huge impact
4	Medical treatments	d	This is already possible on a large production scale

2 Complete the sentences with no more than two words from the text.

1 New _____ cause less environmental damage as they break down after use.

2 Graphene could help with _____ because it has the ability to clear an area of nuclear waste.

3 Filters small enough to remove _____ from seawater could make it drinkable.

4 Graphene can be used to detect and _____ the size of cancer tumours.

5 Graphene could make our terrible _____ on the world smaller.

E Critical thinking

Work in a group. Discuss the questions.

1 Based on the evidence in the text, which development do you think is most likely?

The most likely is probably … because …

2 Many new technologies have unexpected negative effects on the environment. Why do you think this is?

Many new technologies are bad for the environment because …

Study skills | Overcoming writer's block

The following activities can help to overcome writing blocks.

- **Scribble**
  Scribble ideas fast, in any order—whatever comes into your mind—then rearrange what you have written and rewrite it.
- **Write by talking**
  If you find it hard to express yourself in writing, say it out loud and record yourself. Then copy this out and redraft it.
- **Write on loose paper—not in a book**
  If you don't like what you have written, you can throw it away. Alternatively, you can cut it up and rearrange it.

© Stella Cottrell (2013)

1 Work with a partner. Discuss the questions.

   1 How do you generate ideas for an essay?

   2 What do you do if you are struggling to get started?

2 Read the *Overcoming writer's block* box. Does it mention any of the ideas you discussed in Exercise 1?

3 Choose one of the three techniques from the skills box to help you brainstorm ideas for the following essay question.

   There are more challenges and risks than benefits to new technology.

4 Discuss with a partner whether or not you felt the technique helped you generate ideas more easily.

2 READING

New technology: Is greater regulation needed?

A Vocabulary preview

1 Complete the sentences with the words in the box.

concerned   deteriorate   effectively   exaggerate
moral   potential   poverty   stagnant

1 People often _____ how dangerous drones and driverless cars can be.

2 Development can become _____ if companies don't take risks.

3 Companies do not demonstrate _____ behavior when there are large profits to be made.

4 To work _____, companies will increasingly need to use robotics and AI.

5 People should be _____ about the threat to jobs from robotics, but very few are.

6 Robotics has the _____ to dramatically transform today's workplace.

7 Technology should be used to improve the lives of people living in _____.

8 Relationships with others _____ as we become more and more dependent on technology.

2 Check the sentences you agree with in Exercise 1. Compare with a partner.

B Before you read

Activating prior knowledge

Work with a partner. Discuss what you know about each of the following:

artificial intelligence (AI)   big data   driverless cars   robotics

C Global reading

Reading for main ideas

Read *New technology: Is greater regulation needed?* Match the research questions (A–G) to paragraphs (1–7) in the text.

A What is the worst situation from super intelligent robotics?   ____

B What are the risks from big data?   ____

C What are current threats from technology we use?   ____

D What difficult decisions will driverless cars have to make?   ____

E Are there any current worries from robotic developments?   ____

F Are all dangers equal?   ____

G What previous inventions had unknown problems?   ____

New technology:

IS GREATER REGULATION NEEDED?

1 Every time there is a technological revolution the world is transformed. While many of these changes are positive, they are not without their risks. The development of engines transformed world travel, but at the same time it has caused significant environmental damage. Equally, refrigeration has enabled us to preserve food much more effectively, but the CFCs used in the process contributed greatly to global warming. The challenge for governments around the world is the assessment of potential risks and gains—something they haven't always done effectively.

2 These risks are not stagnant from the point of launching a product, but are an ever-evolving challenge that needs constant assessment. People have often worried about the effects of technology on society, and in some cases new laws have emerged as a result of these developments. For example, technology has arguably reduced people's levels of privacy, and laws have been introduced to help combat this. It could also be argued that modern technology has allowed for the rapid spread of misinformation, or "fake news" as it's come to be known. As a result, trust has been lowered and some feel that this has even affected democracy around the world. While there are challenges in monitoring the risks associated with existing technologies, this is an even more difficult task when assessing products and technologies that are still in the early stages of development.

3 One area with huge potential, but also serious risks, is the development of artificial intelligence and robotics. The scenario of machines being more intelligent than people and becoming a danger to society has been frequently portrayed in movies. Academics and high-profile members of the technology industry, such as Stephen Hawking and Bill Gates, have also warned of the dangers of increasingly intelligent AI. Yet for many, these risks are exaggerated to such an extent that it is like worrying about the future overpopulation of humans on another planet. While we are still decades away from robots having human-like intelligence, or even superhuman intelligence, there are some obvious and imminent threats to society.

4 One very immediate worry is that AI could lead to increased inequality and greater levels of unemployment. Professor Moshe Vardi, from Rice University in Texas, has argued that we're not far from a point at which machines will be capable of doing any job a human can. The World Economic Forum has predicted that by 2020, five million jobs in 15 developed countries will be lost due to increased dependence on robotics. In research by the University of Oxford's policy school, nearly half of all jobs in the U.S.A., and three quarters of jobs in China, are at risk from increased automation. There will likely be fewer jobs to compete for, and those that are available are likely to require a high level of education. Consequently, the gap between the rich and the poor will have deteriorated in just a few years. While the threat to jobs is imminent, there are other potential risks further down the line that we do not fully understand. Despite this threat, few governments regulate the use of robotics or create laws to protect jobs.

5 As more of our life, and the things we use, become connected by the Internet, the more data there is out there for companies and organizations to analyze. Big data has huge benefits such as decoding DNA, reducing the energy cost of buildings, and predicting the development of diseases. However, some people are increasingly concerned about how this data is being used. Data could be used to influence how people vote, and ultimately control the decisions people make. The risk therefore comes not from the data itself, but from the person using it and their purpose. Theft, fraud, and even political manipulation are real risks that continually rise as more data is produced and analyzed. In some recent elections, there have been suggestions that governments used big data to influence voters. As a result, it is difficult to see how this could be effectively controlled.

6 Another future concern is the large number of companies who are investing a lot of time and money into developing driverless cars. If all driverless cars were perfect, and all cars on the road had this same technology, then undoubtedly our roads would be safer. However, cars will not only have to be able to do the basics of sensing where other cars are, maintaining appropriate speeds, and other issues of safety, but they will also need to make moral decisions. For example, which direction should a car turn when one way results in killing a child in the road and the other sends the car over the edge of a bridge killing everyone in it?

One challenge here is that the first company to market often makes significantly more money. Take Microsoft with computer operating systems and Apple's iPhone. While unlikely, due to government regulations, the race to get the first driverless car on the road potentially places many lives at risk.

7 It's vital that our evaluation of emerging technologies weighs the potential benefits against the possible risks. Some have the obvious risk of potentially endangering lives if they are pushed forward too quickly. Equally, if the process is well regulated and managed, the same developments could save thousands of lives every year. Other developments are arguably only dangerous in the wrong hands. One thing that is a certain and pressing danger, though, is the increased use of robotics and AI to complete many tasks humans do. While the dream might be that this eliminates the need to work and gives people more leisure time, the reality is that it is also likely to increase inequality and leave vast numbers of people in unemployed poverty.

GLOSSARY

imminent (adj) likely or certain to happen very soon

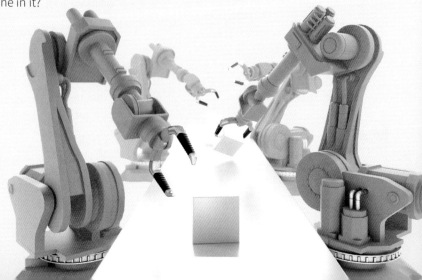

D Close reading

> Many texts conclude with a prediction about the future. However, some texts make predictions throughout. Identifying future structures, paying attention to the use of modals, and adjectives / adverbs to show stance can help you assess how likely the author thinks an idea is.

1   Read *New technology: Is greater regulation needed?* again. Does the author think each of these situations is *L* (Likely) or *U* (Unlikely)?

   1   Robots becoming dangerous and more intelligent than people   ___

   2   Robots taking people's jobs   ___

   3   Big data being used for crime and to negatively influence people   ___

   4   Deaths from driverless cars   ___

2   Read the text again. Do the following statements agree with the ideas expressed by the author? Write *Y* (Yes), *N* (No), or *NG* (Not Given).

   1   Risks and benefits have always been evaluated well.   ___

   2   Technological developments have increased the use of accurate information.   ___

   3   In laboratory conditions, some robots can already perform human-like tasks.   ___

   4   People with fewer qualifications are likely to be most affected by robotics.   ___

   5   Big data is a dangerous concept.   ___

   6   Rushing to make a profit from driverless cars could be dangerous.   ___

   7   Robots will enable us to have more free time.   ___

E Critical thinking

Work with a partner. Discuss the questions.

1   Of the emerging technologies mentioned in the text, which ones worry you the most?

   I'm most worried about … because …

2   Whose responsibility is it to regulate new technology?

   I think it's the responsibility of …

3   What are the dangers of technology not being regulated?

   If technology isn't regulated …

Vocabulary development

Science nouns

1 Match the words in bold with the correct definitions.

1 **atom** (n)
2 **cell** (n)
3 **decay** (n)
4 **discovery** (n)
5 **evaluation** (n)
6 **force** (n)
7 **pressure** (n)
8 **source** (n)

a the gradual destruction of something as a result of a natural process

b something that is found, or something new that is learned

c the power that makes an object move or changes the way it moves

d the smallest unit of any substance

e the smallest part of a living structure that can operate as an independent unit

f the cause of a problem, or the place where it began

g the process of thinking carefully about something before making a judgement about its value, importance, or quality

h the amount of force that a gas or liquid produces in an area or container

2 Complete the sentences with words from Exercise 1. Change the form if necessary.

1 Opponents of nuclear power think we should look for a safer, renewable _____ of energy.

2 The heat created by splitting an _____ is used to create energy in a nuclear power plant.

3 All cars are tested to ensure they can withstand the _____ of a major crash.

4 This report aims to provide a balanced _____ of graphene's potential applications.

5 A bacterium is a single _____ organism. Scientists believe some of the next antibiotics could actually be found in the millions of bacteria found in the soil.

6 The _____ of nuclear waste takes thousands of years.

7 Different materials are developed to withstand greater amounts of _____.

8 The _____ of penicillin is thought to be one of the most important scientific breakthroughs of all time.

Academic words

1 Match the words in bold with the correct definitions.

1 **assessment** (n)
2 **derive** (v)
3 **exhibit** (v)
4 **investigation** (n)
5 **isolate** (v)
6 **nuclear** (adj)
7 **regulate** (v)

a the process of making a judgment or forming an opinion, after considering something or someone carefully

b to show a particular feeling, quality, ability, or form of behavior

c relating to the energy released by splitting an atom

d to get a chemical substance from another substance

e the process of trying to find out all the details or facts about something in order to discover who or what caused it or how it happened

f to control an activity, process, or industry officially by using rules

g to separate a substance from others using a scientific process

2 Complete the questions with the words from Exercise 1. Change the form if necessary.

1 Have there been any benefits from the discovery of _____ power?

2 Should governments _____ emerging technologies until the dangers are fully understood?

3 Do you agree that any _____ into product safety should be conducted by an independent, non-profit organization? Why / why not?

4 What is your _____ of driverless cars? Are they the future? Why / why not?

5 Do you think programs such as Siri and Cortana _____ human-like reactions?

6 Many harmful chemicals are _____ from burning fossil fuels. Is the energy produced worth the environmental cost? Why / why not?

7 Andre Geim and Kostya Novoselov received a Nobel Prize for _____ graphene. What discoveries or inventions would you award a Nobel Prize for?

3 Work with a partner. Discuss the questions in Exercise 2.

Critical thinking

Identifying unreasonable assumptions

Assumptions are ideas we believe to be true, often with little or no proof. Sometimes they can be a useful shortcut to the main argument:

Biomass might be the answer to fossil fuels that society has been looking for.

Here the writer assumes readers will agree that society has been looking for an "answer to fossil fuels." This is a reasonable assumption because the issue of fossil fuels running out and needing to be replaced is well known.

However, sometimes writers imply an idea that is unreasonable:

Driverless cars make driving a more enjoyable, convenient experience. Control of the vehicle is fully automated, allowing the driver to relax.

Here, the writer implies that people don't enjoy driving regular cars and find them inconvenient. This is an unreasonable assumption. Many people enjoy driving and don't find it inconvenient. Although the supporting information is accurate (driverless cars *are* fully automated and *do* allow drivers to relax), this is ultimately a weak argument as the main assumption is false.

1 Read the text and check (✓) the implied assumptions the writer is making.

> The decision was not legally binding and only represented just over half of the population's views. However, the government believes it is the best way for the country to proceed. Since they are elected to power and have all of the social, economic, and political data of the country at hand, it is therefore the best decision.

1 All government investments will be ethical and benefit society. ☐
2 Governments are not motivated by profits. ☐
3 The best technologies can be developed by organizations not interested in profit. ☐
4 Governments have better technological knowledge than companies. ☐

2 Work in a group. Read the examples. What are the implied assumptions in each? Are these reasonable or unreasonable assumptions? Why?

1 Many jobs will increasingly be performed by robots. Therefore, more people will become unemployed.

2 Exams place too many people under stress. As a result, coursework should be used to assess students more.

3 People are increasingly easy to contact for work purposes. This means that they are unable to switch off from work and feel increasingly stressed.

Writing model

You are going to learn about using the future perfect simple, and expressing perspective and stance. You are then going to use these to write an essay discussing whether the risks and challenges outweigh the benefits of new technology.

A Analyze

Read the brainstorm. Circle the three ideas you think are most important.

Challenges and risks	Benefits
Unknown pollutants	May solve environmental problems
Possible misuse	Could make everyday tasks easier
Possible deaths	Could be done faster than humans
Loss of jobs	May allow more free time for humans
	May cure diseases

B Model

1   Read the model. Did the writer choose to focus on the same points?

Emerging technology poses both risks and potential benefits for society. The Internet, for example, has arguably caused the closure of many libraries and main-street businesses. Yet, at the same time, thousands of new jobs in other areas have been created. This essay will argue that while there are clearly challenges and risks, their impact is less than the benefits.

Much new technology in the previous 200 years has caused significant environmental damage, largely due to the burning of fossil fuels. However, sustainable energy sources have significantly reduced emissions of greenhouse gases. Now these forms of energy production are cheaper and more efficient, it's quite possible many countries will have given up their reliance on traditional fuels, and will have switched to green energy in the next few decades.

Furthermore, while there is the immediate threat to jobs from increased automation, this challenge is not a new one. Manufacturing has always evolved to reduce the need for human labor. While the perceived benefits of increased leisure time are perhaps unlikely, it is realistic to imagine people taking on new roles. Although robotics will have taken over many traditional human roles in the future, it is likely that humans will simply have found new roles by then.

Lastly, and arguably most significantly, there are the possible medical benefits. Some people believe that technology may eventually be able to detect and diagnose illnesses more effectively than a doctor. While there are, of course, risks in this, technology here could actually save lives. It could also be used to improve operations and the administration of drugs. Medical practices as a whole will have improved due to emerging technology.

In conclusion, while there are some risks from new technologies, the vast majority are beneficial to society. Thanks to new technology, we could potentially live in a society where many aspects of life will have improved dramatically.

2   With a partner, discuss whether or not you are persuaded by the arguments the writer presents in the essay.

Grammar

Future perfect simple

We use the future perfect simple to describe an action that will be finished by a specific time in the future.

Form: *will + have + past participle*

*Government officials say that the country **will have stopped** using fossil fuels by 2050.*

*Medical practices as a whole **will have improved** due to emerging technology.*

We often use the future perfect simple with expressions of time.

*Robotics will have taken over many traditional human roles **in the future**, but it is likely that humans will simply have found new roles **by then**.*

1 Complete the sentences with the future perfect simple form of the verb in parentheses.

   1 By 2025, robots and other machines _____ (take) millions of jobs from humans.

   2 It is likely that people _____ (travel) to another planet by 2100.

   3 Many governments _____ (ban) cars that run on gas from many cities by 2050.

   4 Robots _____ (replace) humans at work. People will just have different roles.

   5 New technology _____ (reduce) flight times by up to half.

2 Use the prompts to write sentences using the future perfect simple.

   1 2025 solar energy is more important than oil

      By 2025, solar energy will have become more important than oil. (become)

   2 2025 research stops food shortages

      _____ (stop)

   3 2030 all electronic devices connect wirelessly

      _____ (companies / connect)

   4 2035 manufacturers replace plastic packaging with biodegradable packaging

      _____ (replace)

   5 2040 DNA maps from birth reduce disease risk.

      _____ (scientists / map)

3 Work with a partner and discuss the predictions on this page. Which ones do you think will be true?

Writing skill

Academic writing mainly uses research, quotes, and statistics to support arguments. However, the writer also shows their position by the language they use. Two important ways are through perspective and stance.

Perspective—the way of looking at a topic (e.g., political, economic, environmental, medical, legal, etc.).

Stance—the author's view based on the evidence. This is shown through various phrases, often adverbs, verbs, and adjectives (e.g., *unlikely, simply not possible, sufficient,* etc.).

1 Complete the table with the correct forms of words.

Adjective	Adverb	Noun
political		
	legally	
		society
ethical		
	financially	
historical		

2 Complete the sentences with the correct form of the words from Exercise 1.

1 The new technology could affect people _____. Those with a lower level of education could be worse off.

2 The technology works, but there are many things to consider _____ before it can be used on the road. New laws will definitely need to be passed.

3 The government has invested a lot of money in this technology, which shows it has a lot of _____ support.

4 _____, technology has always changed people's jobs. Many jobs once done by people are now done by machine.

5 _____ will have changed beyond recognition due to the use of new technology.

6 Governments are worried about the _____ of allowing machines to become doctors. Machines could make decisions that affect people's lives significantly.

Writing task

You are going to write an opinion essay in response to the following:
"There are more challenges and risks than benefits to new technology."

Brainstorm

Use the table to brainstorm the potential risks, challenges, and benefits of new technology.

Risks and challenges	Benefits

Plan

Answer the questions.

1   Are the risks greater than the benefits?
2   Which of the risks is the greatest?
3   Which of the benefits are the most important?

Write

Use your brainstorm and plan to help you write your essay. Remember to use the future perfect simple where appropriate and to show your perspective and stance. Your essay should be 250 words long.

Share

Exchange your essay with a partner. Use the checklist on page 189 to help you provide feedback to your partner.

Rewrite and edit

Consider your partner's comments and write your final draft. Think about:

- whether you answered the question clearly
- whether you used the future perfect simple appropriately
- whether you showed your perspective and stance appropriately.

Review

Wordlist

MACMILLAN DICTIONARY

Vocabulary preview

concerned (adj) ***	filter (n) **	revolutionary (adj) **
deteriorate (v) *	moral (adj) ***	stagnant (adj)
devastating (adj) *	obsolete (adj)	tackle (v) **
effectively (adv) ***	particle (n) **	threat (n) ***
efficiency (n) **	poverty (n) **	
exaggerate (v) *	property (n) ***	

Vocabulary development

atom (n) **	discovery (n) ***	pressure (n) ***
cell (n) ***	evaluation (n)	source (n) ***
decay (n) *	force (n) ***	

Academic words

assessment (n) **	investigation (n) ***	regulate (v) **
derive (v) ***	isolate (v) *	
exhibit (v) **	nuclear (adj) ***	

Academic words review

Complete the sentences with the words in the box.

assessment	code	comprised	derived	isolate

1 Many ideas about future technologies are _____ from science fiction.

2 A decision will be made following the government's _____.

3 Some argue that scientists should follow a strict ethical _____.

4 Fossil fuels are _____ of decayed animals and plants that have been converted to oil or gas.

5 Scientists managed to _____ the chemical from a natural substance.

Unit review

Reading 1	☐ I can identify conclusions and reasons.
Reading 2	☐ I can identify predictions in texts.
Study skill	☐ I can overcome writer's block.
Vocabulary	☐ I can use science nouns.
Writing	☐ I can write persuasive arguments.
Grammar	☐ I can use future perfect simple.

Functional language phrase bank

The phrases below give common ways of expressing useful functions. Use them to help you as you're completing the *Discussion points, Critical thinking* activities, and *Speaking* tasks.

Asking for clarification
Sorry, can you explain that some more?
Could you say that another way?
When you say … do you mean …?
Sorry, I don't follow that.
What do you mean?

Asking for repetition
Could you repeat that, please?
I'm sorry, I didn't catch that.
Could you say that again?

When you don't know the word for something
What does … mean?
Sorry, I'm not sure what … means.

Working with a partner
Would you like to start?
Shall I go first?
Shall we do this one first?
Where do you want to begin?

Giving opinions
I think that …
It seems to me that …
In my opinion …
As I see it …

Agreeing and disagreeing
I know what you mean.
That's true.
You have a point there.
Yes. I see what you're saying, but …
I understand your point, but …
I don't think that's true.

Asking for opinions
Do you think …?
Do you feel …?
What do you think about …?
How about you, Jennifer?
What do you think?
What about you?
Does anyone have any other ideas?
Do you have any thoughts on this?

Asking for more information
In what way?
Why do you think that?
Can you give an example?

Not giving a strong preference
It doesn't matter to me.
I don't really have a strong preference.
I've never really thought about that.
Either is fine.

Expressing interest
I'd like to hear more about that.
That sounds interesting.
How interesting!
Tell me more about that.

Giving reasons
This is … because …
This has to be … because …
I think … because …

Checking understanding
Do you know what I mean?
Do you see what I'm saying?
Are you following me?

Putting things in order
This needs to come first because …
I think this is the most / least important because …
For me, this is the most / least relevant because …

Writing task peer review checklist

Use the checklist below as you read over your partner's work.

1 Does the composition have these things?

- a title

- a clear structure (e.g. an introduction, body, and conclusion)

- appropriate punctuation

2 Write the thesis statement here:

_____

3 Underline the topic sentences in each paragraph. Write the number of any paragraphs that don't have a clear topic sentence here:

_____

4 Is the author's position on the issue / topic clear?

5 Have they included any vocabulary from the unit? If so, is it used appropriately?

6 Have they used any grammar from the unit? If so, it is used appropriately?

7 Underline any sentences or passages you particularly like. What do you like about them?

8 Are sources provided for factual statements?

9 Are claims or arguments supported by evidence?

10 Write one question about the content for the author:

_____

Academic words revision

Units 1–5

Complete the sentences using the words in the box.

> abandon   acknowledge   categories   complex   journal
> outcome   overseas   purchase   regulation   tradition

1   Mathematical formulas are too _____ for most children.

2   The weather was so bad that we had to _____ the building work completely.

3   The oil company will start drilling as soon as they _____ the land.

4   This kind of pottery is now popular _____ as well as in this country.

5   Unfortunately, the federal government failed to _____ their responsibility in this matter.

6   The ability to sort things into _____ is evidence of logic.

7   Thanks to the new _____, the number of forest fires has been in decline.

8   Unfortunately, the study had no significant _____.

9   The _____ decided not to publish the results of the study as they felt it wasn't comprehensive enough.

10 Japanese _____ shows that imperfect objects can be beautiful.

Units 6–10

Complete the sentences using the words in the box.

> clause   device   discrimination   distribution   exhibit
> investigation   phenomenon   regulate   thereby   transmission

1   Vaccinations provide one method of preventing the _____ of diseases.

2   Governments should _____ the use of all new technologies.

3   Humans _____ a huge variety of behaviors.

4   Unfortunately, there are still many social groups that face _____.

5   The _____ of information today is faster and wider than ever before.

6   There is a new _____ that will make communication even more efficient.

7   There is a _____ in the contract which states that employees must not share any information with the company's competitors.

8   A tsunami is just one example of a naturally occurring _____.

9   A new chemical has recently been isolated, _____ improving scientists' chances of developing the new drug.

10 The research department carried out an _____ into how artificial intelligence technologies will affect our lives.

Macmillan Education Limited
4 Crinan Street
London N1 9XW

Companies and representatives throughout the world

ISBN 978-1-380-00596-0

Text, design and illustration © Macmillan Education Limited 2018

Written by Louis Rogers and Dorothy E. Zemach
Series Consultant Dorothy E. Zemach
The author has asserted their right to be identified as the author of this work in accordance with the Copyright, Designs and Patents Act 1988.

This edition published 2018
First edition entitled "Skillful" published 2012 by Macmillan Education Limited

Designed by emc design ltd
Illustrated by Carl Morris (Beehive Illustration) pp64, 69, 93 and 96.
Cover design by emc design ltd
Cover picture by Sam Parij (Eye Candy Illustration)/Getty Images/Moment Open/
Alicia Llop
Picture research by Emily Taylor

The publishers would like to thank the following for their thoughtful insights and perceptive comments during the development of the material:

Dalal Al Hitty, University of Bahrain, Bahrain; Karin Heuert Galvão, i-Study Interactive Learning, São Paulo, Brazil; Ohanes Sakris, Australian College of Kuwait, Kuwait; Eoin Jordan, Xi'an Jiaotong-Liverpool University, Suzhou, China; Aaron Rotsinger, Xi'an Jiaotong-Liverpool University, Suzhou, China; Dr. Osman Z. Barnawi, Royal Commission Yanbu Colleges & Institutes, Yanbu, Saudi Arabia; Andrew Lasher, SUNY Korea, Incheon, South Korea; Fatoş Uğur Eskiçırak, Bahçeşehir University, Istanbul, Turkey; Dr. Asmaa Awad, University of Sharjah, Sharjah, United Arab Emirates; Amy Holtby, The Petroleum Institute, Abu Dhabi, United Arab Emirates; Dr. Christina Gitsaki, Zayed University, Dubai, United Arab Emirates.

The author and publishers would like to thank the following for permission to reproduce their images

Cover Image Getty Images/Ali Llop; **Alamy**/Biosphoto p155(inset), Alamy/Blend Images p119, Alamy/Chronicle p101(bl), Alamy/dieKleinert p83(tl), Alamy/Hero Images p142, Alamy/Nobeastsofierce Science p173, Alamy/Scenics p124(cm), Alamy/Shotshop p141, Alamy/Timsimagesunderwater p155, Alamy/Zoonar p47; **Corbis** p69; **Getty Images**/AFP Creative p134-135, Getty Images/AsiaPac pp98-99, 170-171, Getty Images/Caiaimage p51(t), Getty Images/Dan Barnes p80-81, Getty Images/Blend Images p164, Getty Images/DeAgostini p29(tl), Getty Images/Digital Vision p105, Getty Images/EyeEm/Martin Jordan p175, Getty Images/Kathleen Finlay p106, Getty Images/Flash Parker p8-9, Getty Images/Gilaxia p34, Getty Images/Alma Haser p16, Getty Images/Anna Hedderly p29(background), Getty Images/iStockphoto p137, Getty Images/iStockPhoto/BahadirTanriover p177, Getty Images/iStockPhoto/Thomas Faull p154(tl), Getty Images/iStockPhoto/Johnny Greig p40, Getty Images/iStockPhoto/IlonaBudzbon p101(tr), Getty Images/iStockPhoto/Jamesteohart p123, Getty Images/iStockphoto/Kyoshino p29(br), Getty Images/iStock/PeopleImages p15, Getty Images/iStockPhoto/Pinkypills p160, Getty Images/iStockPhoto/Bernhard_Staehli p89, Getty Images/iStockPhoto/John Verner p33(tr), Getty Images/Jenner Images p12, Getty Images/Adrian Koehli p56, Getty Images/Barry Kusuma p37, Getty Images/Lonely Planet Images p83(br), Getty Images/Los Angeles Times p62-63, Getty Images/Maskot p121, Getty Images/Mint Images p65, Getty Images/Moment p87, Getty Images/Nature Picture Library p70, Getty Images/Nick Obank/Barcroft Media p152-153, Getty Images/PeopleImages p52, Getty Images/Science Photo Library pp19, 154(bl), 178, Getty Images/The Image Bank p33(tl), Getty Images/Westend61 p11, Getty Images/Westphalia p88, Getty Images/Yangna p124(b); **PlainPicture**/Cavan Images p116-117, Plain Picture/Valery Skurydin p26-27; **Science Photo Library**/James King-Holmes p44-45; **Shutterstock** p51(cm); **Thomson Reuters** pp8, 26, 44, 62, 80, 98, 116, 134, 152, 170.

These materials may contain links for third party websites. We have no control over, and are not responsible for, the contents of such third party websites. Please use care when accessing them.

Printed and bound in Poland by CGS

2024 2023 2022 2021 2020
24 23 22 21 20 19 18 17 16 15

PALGRAVE STUDY SKILLS

by bestselling author, **Stella Cottrell**

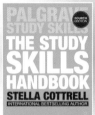 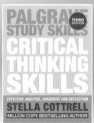 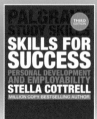 

  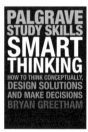   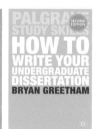

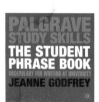   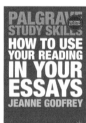 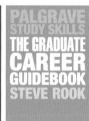 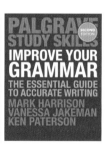

palgravestudyskills.com

 facebook.com/skills4study

twitter.com/skills4study